FOOTNOTES TO HISTORY

Father E.A. Walsh, S.J. in his favorite environment--a map and an audience.

FOOTNOTES TO HISTORY:

SELECTED SPEECHES AND WRITINGS OF EDMUND A. WALSH, S.J.

FOUNDER OF THE SCHOOL OF FOREIGN SERVICE

Edited with Commentary by
Anna Watkins

Introduction by
Walter I. Giles

Published for the Georgetown University
School of Foreign Service
70th Anniversary
1919–1989

Georgetown University Press
Washington, D.C.

Excerpts from *Total Power* by Edmund A. Walsh, S.J. copyright 1948 by Edmund A. Walsh. Reprinted by permission of Doubleday & Company, Inc.

Excerpt from *The Fall of the Russian Empire* by Edmund A. Walsh, S.J., Ph.D. copyright 1927, 1928 by Edmund A. Walsh. Reprinted by permission of Little, Brown and Company.

Copyright © 1990 by Georgetown University Press

Printed in the United States of America

All rights reserved

Library of Congress Cataloging-in-Publication Data

Walsh, Edmund A. (Edmund Aloysius), 1885-1956.
    Footnotes to history.

    "Published for the Georgetown University School of Foreign Service, 70th anniversary, 1919-1989."
    Includes bibliographical references.
    1. World politics--1945-   . 2. International relations.   3. Geopolitics. 4. First strike (Nuclear strategy)   I. Watkins, Anna. II. Georgetown University. School of Foreign Service.   III. Title.
D843.W332 1989   327'.09'045   89-25904
ISBN 0-87840-506-2

Contents

Preface	vii
Introduction	1

PART I: RUSSIA … 19

1. Sic Transit Gloria Mundi … 21
2. Soviet Russia and the Peace of Europe … 41
3. Communism and the Soviet Threat to Democracy … 57

PART II: INTERNATIONAL RELATIONS … 71

4. See Life Steadily and See It Whole … 73
5. The Future of Pan–American Relations … 83

PART III: GEOPOLITICS … 93

6. Germany's Master Geopolitician … 95
7. Russian Geopolitics and the United States … 129

PART IV: IS IT IMMORAL TO STRIKE FIRST? … 141

8. Is It Immoral to Strike First If Attack Is Imminent? … 143

PART V: IN HONOR OF GREAT MEN … 151

9. A Sermon from a Stained Glass Window … 153
10. William Gaston of North Carolina … 159

Chronology of Father Walsh's Life … 173

Preface

In 1986, when engaged in research for one of my papers as a graduate student at Georgetown University, I came across the treasure of Father Walsh's papers stored in the Special Collections Division of Lauinger Library. A cursory review of these manuscripts piqued my curiosity; further examination revealed Father Walsh's wide range of interests and his engaging literary style replete with anecdotes and quotations from many fields. Father Walsh's ideas and views were well known in his time, when he was recognized as a world authority on Russian affairs and expert on geopolitics. Despite their grounding in his own times, his speeches and writings retain remarkable freshness, and some of the topics he discussed still occupy our minds today.

I became convinced that this buried treasure should be unearthed so that others could benefit from his writings, and have an opportunity to reminisce about this outstanding scholar. The seventieth anniversary of the School of Foreign Service in 1989 seemed a fitting occasion for the publication of his writings. Dr. Peter F. Krogh, dean of the School, agreed to my proposal to publish a selection of Father Walsh's speeches and written works.

In selecting for this publication from an abundance of material—42 boxes with 200 folders on a wide range of issues—I was guided by topical diversity. I intended to reflect Father Walsh's main areas of interest as they seem to have developed over his lifetime. The two last lectures were included for their special significance to all connected with Georgetown. Professor Walter I. Giles contributed to the final selection of topics.

As to the editorial method, in general, the texts are as Father Walsh wrote them, with the addition of passages from sources he indicated in his manuscripts. In some instances, sentences or paragraphs were excised to avoid repitition or rearranged to achieve clarity. In other cases, factual inconsistencies were corrected and the punctuation was changed. Furthermore, adaptations were needed to change the spoken word to written language. In many places, Father Walsh refers to "Russia" instead of using the postrevolutionary "Soviet Union," but the reader can readily see where to make the mental substitution. The introductory notes on each selection grew out of the editor's own researches for this volume.

I am profoundly grateful to Professors Dorothy M. Brown, John B. Breslin, S.J. and Francis X. Winters, S.J. for their encouragement, support, and practical assistance, particularly in the early stages of the project, and their continuous interest in its development. I also wish to thank Margery Boichel, editor of the Institute for the Study of Diplomacy, for her valuable suggestions regarding the presentation of the text.

My special thanks go to the staff of the Special Collections Division and of the Reference Department of Lauinger Library for their unstinting assistance in providing background material as well as factual information. I also acknowledge the permission of Little, Brown and Company and Doubleday & Company, Inc., to use copyrighted material from Father Walsh's books, *The Fall of the Russian Empire* and *Total Power*.

Anna Watkins

Introduction

The publication of this anthology during the seventieth year of the Edmund A. Walsh School of Foreign Service represents, in the opinion of the writer,[1] a most appropriate memorial to the founder of this internationally renowned educational institution. During the first three decades of the School's existence—almost half of its entire life—it reflected, in a manner rarely experienced in our own times, the genius and creativity of one of the most gifted and indeed charismatic personalities of the Society of Jesus in the twentieth century: Edmund A. Walsh. It was not surprising that after the death of Father Walsh in 1956, the University renamed the School in honor of its founder.

Seldom has the cliché—"a legend in his own time"—been truer than it was of Edmund Walsh. Although a number of Jesuits have left their mark on Georgetown University during the first half of this century, none of them achieved the national eminence of his rich and varied career. Scholar, writer, teacher, educator, political commentator and advocate, Vatican diplomat, American government official—all of these roles were discharged by Father Walsh at one time or another during a life filled with an extraordinary diversity of personal achievement and public service. For thousands of graduates of Georgetown University, the name "Father Walsh" has been long synonymous with their Alma Mater, and especially with the School of Foreign Service.

It is hoped, therefore, that this volume of selected writings, lectures, and public addresses of Father Walsh will serve to recall the impressive career of this remarkable man and bring into somewhat clearer focus the impact he had on the world, the nation, Washington, and on Georgetown over many years. Moreover, it is the belief of Dean Peter F. Krogh, who encouraged the editor of this volume and made possible its publication during this anniversary, that the book itself will be another deserved tribute to the memory of the remarkable founder of this celebrated institution.

Before commenting on the individual selections of this anthology, I believe the reader's interest in these materials will be enhanced by an understanding of the historical and educational roles which fully occupied Father Walsh's life. A detailed biographical chronology of the principal developments in Father Walsh's career has been compiled by the editor of this volume, Mrs. Anna Watkins, and is found on page 173 of the book. My introduction, accordingly, will sketch the context of Edmund Walsh's career and appraise his accomplishments chiefly from the perspective of the events which shaped the history of Walsh's own times. And thus the various writings and addresses selected for this volume may be considered historical footnotes documenting in part the career of this remarkable priest.

When Edmund Walsh died at the age of seventy-one, *The Washington Post* of November 3, 1956 editorialized that the capital had lost "one of its most influential figures." Father Walsh, observed the *Post*, "was a man of prodigious energy, of great intellectual vigor, of handsome and impressive appearance, a prolific writer and a most accomplished lecturer and public speaker." The influence exerted by Father Walsh, to which the *Post* editorial alluded, derives in part, if not entirely, from two major roles this Jesuit priest played throughout his life. First, as a student of the Russian Revolution, and an analyst of the Soviet political system which followed it, Father Walsh became a national figure in educating the American public and its political leaders to the threat posed by international communism to the democracies of the West, a threat spearheaded by the Soviet Union. Second, Father Walsh achieved national recognition as a pioneering and innovative educator. His founding of the School of Foreign Service in 1919, and his subsequent development and direction of that School for more than thirty years, enhanced his reputation, not simply as a prominent educator, but also as an influential player in the Washington political world. The School was, and remained for many years, the only institution in the nation designed specifically to train its students for diplomatic and consular careers as well as for positions in the private sectors of international trade and transportation.

Both of these roles, one political, the other educational, brought national attention to Father Walsh. They made him an influential figure, but a controversial one as well. The controversy surrounding Father Walsh as a consequence of his unrelenting opposition to the Soviet regime is a matter of public record.[2] The controversial aspects of his role as an innovative Jesuit educator have not previously been publicized but they are, I think, no less interesting and significant for the history of the Georgetown School of Foreign Service than the public controversies.

Father Walsh's scholarly and political interests in Soviet politics and international communism began early in his life, during the years 1922-23, when he headed the Papal Famine Relief Mission to Russia. That firsthand experience with the new revolutionary order in Russia led to his becoming a student of the Russian Revolution and of the subsequent communist regime. It also led to his preoccupation with Marxist ideology and with communist theories of world domination by the USSR.

Walsh's opposition to American recognition of the Bolshevik government in Soviet Russia, expressed in numerous writings and hundreds of public lectures, addresses, and private conversations with members of Washington's political elite, brought him national recognition and influence in the corridors of the capital's political establishment. Some of that influence came from his many professional and social contacts with high-ranking executive, legislative, and diplomatic officials. He was conceded to be a powerful proponent of the U.S. government's policy of nonrecognition of the Soviet government which prevailed from the overthrow of the

Kerensky government in 1917. That particular influence proved unavailing, however, with the new Roosevelt administration in 1933 when it brought about, over the vigorous opposition of Father Walsh and others, the diplomatic recognition of the Soviet Union. Despite this break with the White House, Walsh succeeded in maintaining considerable behind-the-scenes political influence in Washington.

His several diplomatic missions abroad in behalf of the Vatican contributed to his reputation as a knowledgeable and authoritative scholar in the arena of international diplomacy. He also had important ties with leading businessmen. His own "political base," the School of Foreign Service itself, provided Walsh with both prestige and an academic format congenial to his personal political interests. He continued to be a much sought after public speaker, as well as a private advisor, on many kinds of international issues in the years prior to, during, and after World War II.

With the coming of the Truman administration in 1945, the advent of the Cold War, the promulgation of the Truman Doctrine and other American foreign policies which sought to contain the Soviet Union and the spread of international communism, Father Walsh again became a welcome figure in White House circles. By the time of his death in 1956, world events had corroborated his views of the historic significance of the Russian Revolution and the international political developments which followed from that "tragic" event, as Walsh always maintained it to be.

Father Walsh's role in opposing the Soviet Union and the expansion of communism beyond the borders of that state made him an implacable enemy in the eyes of the radical left. He was also suspect to many, but not all, American liberals who were themselves divided on American policy towards the Soviet Union.

Opposition to Walsh's anti-Soviet political advocacy was sometimes directed towards his School of Foreign Service. The School was, as they perceived it, a *Roman Catholic* institution, presumably inculcating hundreds of future American government and business officials not only with Walsh's doctrinaire opposition to the Soviet Union but also with other doctrines and attitudes, of a reactionary and conservative nature, thought to prevail within many Catholic Church circles.

The second role in the life of Edmund Walsh, a role which brought him educational distinction at a national level, was his founding in 1919, at the age of thirty-four, of the School of Foreign Service and his subsequent direction of that institution during most of his active life. The historical and descriptive facts about Georgetown's School of Foreign Service are well known, especially to the readers of the present volume as most of them are either alumni, students, or friends of this institution. But Walsh's School of Foreign Service, it should be remembered, was highly innovative educationally for its time. It proved to be a precursor of significant educational developments in the academic study of international relations and the practice of diplomacy, that would take place in many of the nation's leading academic institutions only after World War II, almost a quarter of a century after Walsh founded his School.

In 1919, the concept of international relations as a distinct academic discipline hardly existed. Only a few universities offered graduate studies in international law and relations, and even fewer courses existed on the undergraduate level. "Majors" in international relations, international law, foreign policy and diplomacy did not exist. The United States diplomatic and consular service itself, later to be reorganized as the Foreign Service of the United States, had yet to develop a professionalized corps. And isolationist thinking was rampant. It was in this rather unfavorable political and educational environment that Walsh, convinced that the United States was destined to play an important political and economic role in world affairs, and with the active backing of Father John B. Creeden, S.J., then President of the University, and the strong support of the Maryland Provincial of the Society of Jesus, founded the Georgetown School of Foreign Service. The School was officially inaugurated on November 25, 1919. From that time until late 1952, Father

Walsh directed the development of what would soon be recognized nationally as a unique institution of higher learning in the United States.[3]

The School was unusual in being the first American institution of higher learning devoted entirely to the study and practice of international relations, international trade and transportation. Moreover, an undergraduate college whose curriculum was built predominantly around the social sciences, law, modern languages, geography, and various vocational specializations was, in 1919, a significant departure from the classical and liberal arts curriculum then characteristic of the typical Jesuit college in the United States.

But this radical departure did not come about without difficulty or criticism. Walsh was controversial to some members of the Georgetown community for two distinct, although closely related, reasons. First, his professional lifestyle and his prominence as a political commentator made him an unconventional Jesuit for his period, when it was virtually unheard of for a member of the Catholic clergy to be a political activist in the public forum.[4] Many of Walsh's professional endeavors involved nonreligious interests—concerns which seemed not to be the proper agenda for an American Jesuit. He was privately criticized by some Jesuits because of his political visibility, and because they assumed that his primary personal concerns were essentially worldly. In sum, Walsh's critics within the Jesuit order and the broader Georgetown community thought he lacked the kind of spirituality, and commitment to strictly religious interests and activities, deemed appropriate at that time for a Catholic priest.

In addition, the extensive national press publicity which Walsh received throughout his life was perceived by those critics, rightly or wrongly, to constitute an exploitation of his status and position, both as a Jesuit and as a Georgetown administrator. Some complained that far too much public attention was directed to Walsh's career personally rather than to the University as an institution.

It is undoubtedly difficult for the contemporary observer to understand the attitudes of a bygone era which viewed with disfavor a Catholic clergyman extensively pursuing political interests rather than religious ones. Since the 1960s, at least, many members of the clergy, from all denominations, have been intensively and publicly involved in many controversial events, in all aspects of American politics, domestic and foreign. Such activities, although sometimes criticized here and there, do not evoke today the kind of disparagement and opposition which often was the case during the time of Walsh. Even when his highly visible political activities involved the advocacy of political policies and attitudes strongly held by most American Catholics, i.e., anti-Soviet Union and anti-international communism, they were not appreciated by some of his Jesuit colleagues at Georgetown. Their critical views, of course, were expressed privately.

The second controversial issue in the career of Father Walsh at Georgetown concerned *his* School of Foreign Service. The School itself entirely reflected Walsh's philosophy of a curriculum designed to achieve the School's professional objectives, and to do so more as a national, nonsectarian institution of higher learning, rather than as a Catholic one. Granted that the School was from the outset a unique institution, that it did soon acquire considerable prestige and fame, that it resulted in a tremendous amount of favorable publicity for the entire University of which it was a part; still, the School of Foreign Service was not accepted by a number of influential Jesuits on the Georgetown campus during Walsh's lifetime. Tolerated, yes, but not really accepted. There is a critical difference.

Indeed, the favorable national publicity which the School received often served to increase the reservations of a number of Jesuits for the institution. To them the School of Foreign Service represented not simply a radical break with traditional Jesuit educational principles; it was also perceived as a worldly, nonreligious undergraduate institution, engaged in competition for academic recognition with the College of Arts and Sciences and its classical liberal arts curricula. And although the site of the School had been moved (in the early 1930s, from its previous location in the Law School in downtown Washington) to the main campus, the institution was often referred to by its critics as "the foreign school." And it was not without significance that no Jesuit priest, other than Father Walsh himself, and a Jesuit colleague who taught the obligatory religion course for the School's Catholic students, was a continuing member of the faculty of the School of Foreign Service during most of the institution's first three decades.[5] Instead, there was the overwhelming presence of a dynamic and charismatic figure, Father Walsh himself, a presence not associated with any particular religious significance even though he was a member of a religious order.

The strengths and the weaknesses of the School, and indeed its very existence, seemed to many observers, both within and outside the Georgetown community, to be wrapped up entirely in the personal leadership of Father Walsh. While he directed the institution, the School of Foreign Service was secure from its critics on the Hilltop. But after his death in 1956, the future of the institution was in some doubt for a number of years.

Those apprehensions and fears about the permanent existence or vitality of the School of Foreign Service were never realized, in spite of this period of drift. In addition, the former ideological arguments on the campus concerning the very concept of an undergraduate school of foreign service—that is, whether it was a valid or an aberrational educational program—also ceased. The School is no longer simply tolerated at Georgetown, as it was for many years; it now occupies a major, dynamic and respected role in the functioning of the University at large.

This is the reality of the Edmund A. Walsh School of Foreign Service today: its historical endurance and present vitality some three decades after the death of its founder. And that reality is, in my opinion, the most deserved and appropriate tribute which can be rendered to the memory of Father Edmund Walsh in this seventieth year of the life of the School he founded.

These "Footnotes to History," named after the title in part of one of Father Walsh's own books, contain only a fraction of the thousands of pages of published works and unpublished public addresses and lectures which came from his pen. He was a most prolific writer and a frequent and eloquent public speaker. As this book's title suggests, what is set out between its covers are simply "selections" from the voluminous materials which Mrs. Anna Watkins, the meticulous and indefatigable researcher of the Walsh Papers at Georgetown, has read, often reconstructed in part, organized, and finally edited. Father Walsh's interests centered primarily on the Russian Revolution, communism, Soviet foreign policy, international communism, international politics, American diplomacy, international trade, geopolitics, and occasional Catholic humanistic studies. This anthology accurately reflects those interests.

Preceding the text of each selection, the editor has prepared an introductory note which delineates the historical background of the particular topic. She has also grouped these materials into five general categories according to their subject matters. The first selection of Part I, Russia, to which the editor has given the title "Sic Transit Gloria Mundi," consists of two chapters taken from Father Walsh's book, *The Fall of the Russian Empire: The Story of the Last of the Romanovs and the Coming of the Bolsheviki*, first published in 1928 and reprinted several times. It was one of the first histories of these events published in the United States. These chapters reflect Father Walsh's talent as a consummate storyteller, excelling when his historical materials involved dramatic and tragic events.

The second selection, "Soviet Russia and the Peace of Europe," articulates Father Walsh's lifelong belief that the "ultimate goal" of Soviet foreign policy "may reasonably be deduced from the fundamental dogmas" of Marxism which have never been repudiated, was both a prophetic and a courageous speech. In 1944, American idealism concerning the postwar policies and aims of the USSR was at its apogee. The conventional wisdom of mainstream establishment commentary at the time assumed that the international order after the war would be characterized by relations of friendship, cooperation, and collaboration between the wartime allies, the United States and the Soviet Union. To express public skepticism of that assumption was to risk the "absurd contention," as Walsh observed, "that he who criticizes communism at present is giving aid and solace to Hitler."

Walsh's lecture asserts that the Soviet Union's postwar foreign policy would be guided by considerations of *realpolitik*, not by the idealistic expressions of enduring friendship and cooperation with the United States which abounded at that time. Walsh predicted that after the war the USSR would seek aggressively to enlarge its sphere of influence in Europe both geographically and ideologically and "expand a way of life hostile to Christianity and Democracy...." Within three years of this address, the Cold War between the United States and the USSR had begun. Walsh's skepticism of, and warnings about, the Soviets had already proved to be correct.

"Communism and the Soviet Threat to Democracy," the final selection in Part I, constitutes an unequivocal reaffirmation of Walsh's long held views on the potential danger posed to world peace by the Soviet Union, which had been understandably muted somewhat and expressed in guarded language in his public pronouncements during the World War II period.

Analyzing the world situation as it existed in 1947, Walsh asserted that the failed attempt of Nazi Germany to impose a dictatorial hegemony on the world had been succeeded by a similar attempt of the Soviet Union, which, he said, "now stands, in full armor, knocking at the door of the West."

Part II, International Relations, contains two selections representative of Walsh's many writings and public addresses concerning American diplomacy and the appropriate factors of a foreign policy designed to promote a stable and just international order. The first of these addresses, "See Life Steadily and See It Whole," blends a variety of subjects: the importance of morality, idealism, law and justice in the relations between sovereign nations; the fusion in American foreign policy of both idealistic commitments and *realpolitik*;

the gradual attainment of international peace; the view that a general war in Europe, if it should come, would leave communism and the parties of the Left as the only victors; and the belief that a just international society must secure and protect the "sovereign rights of the smallest republic...."

It also reflected Walsh's views on the role of international relations in higher education, that general humanistic studies should form a major component of the educational training of American diplomats. The emphasis which Walsh placed on international law and international justice as vital factors in American foreign policy during this period contrasts somewhat with his later themes of power politics and military power as the *sine qua non* of American diplomacy and American security. This different emphasis may be explained, I believe, by the fact that in 1934, when the Delaware address was delivered, Hitler's dictatorship was just emerging, the Soviet Union was not yet a world military power, its domestic situation was turbulent and depressed, and it seemingly posed no immediate threat to Western or even Eastern Europe despite the international revolutionary fervor of its Marxist ideology. Finally, dominant opinion in the United States with respect to foreign policy and national security interests tended to reflect idealistic concepts of international law, organization and collective security (the League of Nations syndrome, for example), as well as the belief that the United States should, and could, maintain a splendid hemispheric isolation from the problems of Europe and Asia.

The second selection placed in Part II is Walsh's lecture on "The Future of Pan-American Relations," delivered in 1944. Although U.S. relations with the Latin American republics were not a primary concern in American foreign policy during Walsh's lifetime, Latin American studies had long been included in the curriculum of the School of Foreign Service. "The Future of Pan-American Relations" ranges over a number of factors which, in Walsh's opinion, had historically influenced this country's relations with the republics to the south and which should be reckoned with in the future if the United States's post-World War II ties with

Latin America were to be grounded on a just and stable basis.

The contemporary reader will undoubtedly note that Walsh said virtually nothing about the possibility that the social, economic, and political environment in Latin America could become a seed bed of Marxist ideological revolutionary movements, Soviet-style, in the future. Walsh, who would otherwise be extremely sensitive to the matter, did not address it simply because Latin America was assumed at the time to be politically insulated from the powerful ideological currents then coursing through Europe. In addition, the national security interests of the United States during the 1930s and 1940s were conceived almost entirely in terms of this country's relations with Europe, the Soviet Union, and Asia.

The two selections in Part III, Geopolitics, represent Father Walsh's primary academic and political interests during the last decade of his active public life. Geopolitics as an academic study had been a part of the curriculum of the School of Foreign Service for a number of years before Walsh made it his foremost academic concern during the World War II years. He not only taught courses and seminars in geopolitics, with emphasis on the Germanic version, but also lectured frequently on the subject throughout the country, especially at some of the U.S. military schools and officer training institutions. It was a subject attuned to the national security and foreign policy concerns of the nation during the war. Nazi Germany, and not Soviet Russia or international communism, was the immediate military threat to the United States.

Walsh's involvement with this somewhat exotic geographical-political-military subject further enhanced his reputation within American military circles as a hard-headed realist in international politics. It was not surprising that his visibility as a leading scholar and commentator on German geopolitics led to his appointment, in 1945, as a consultant to the United States Chief of Counsel for the Nuremberg War Crimes Trials, Supreme Court Justice Robert H. Jackson. The particular mission of Father Walsh was to interrogate Germany's "master geopolitician," Dr. Karl Haushofer, to determine whether this prominent and influential proponent of German geopolitics should be charged with criminal liability at the Nuremberg trials.

Walsh's studies and teaching of geopolitics and his personal and official associations with Karl Haushofer in Germany after the war, led to his book, *Total Power: A Footnote to History*, published in 1948. The editor has given the two chapters included in the present volume the collective title of "Germany's Master Geopolitician." The first selection (chapter 4 in *Total Power*) contains Walsh's dramatic account of the last days and suicide of Professor General Haushofer and his wife. Chapter 5 is titled "Last Will and Testament of German Geopolitics." It deals generally with the influence of geographical factors on international politics as well as with Haushofer's own geopolitical theories, which often supported Hitler's philosophy of German territorial expansion and European domination. Overall, "Last Will and Testament of German Geopolitics" is a somewhat funereal summing up of the demise of German geopolitics following the Nazi defeat in World War II.

In one of his last public lectures, "Russian Geopolitics and the United States," the other selection in Part III, Father Walsh brought together the two central political interests which had preoccupied him during the last years of his professional career: the postwar expansion of Soviet communism throughout Europe, with its threat to the security of the United States and other Western democracies, and the Soviet use of German geopolitics as an intellectual instrument to promote the Kremlin's ultimate objective of world domination.

In December 1950, when Father Walsh wrote the article "Is It Immoral to Strike First if Attack is Imminent?" for the Washington newspaper, *The Sunday Star* (Part IV of the anthology), the subject of nuclear warfare had become not only a major military strategic concern for the United States but also a moral dilemma of extreme complexity and sensitivity for a democratic and religious nation. As long as only this country possessed a monopoly on the awesome atomic weapons which had been successfully used against Japan in 1945, the question of the ethical problems resulting from the employment of such lethal weapons remained abstract. But by late 1950, when Walsh's article appeared, the USSR was on the eve of producing atomic weapons itself.

The military problem of the use of nuclear weapons was far more complicated for the political leaders of the United States than it was for the Soviet rulers. American historical practice, as well as the predominant religious teachings prevailing in this country, recoiled from the proposition that the initiation of war by the United States alone, through a surprise attack on another nation, could be morally justifiable. And when the surprise attack might be in the form of a preemptive nuclear strike, thereby unleashing a holocaust of almost unimaginable destruction, the moral dimensions of such a strategic military policy were magnified beyond compare.

Father Walsh defended the morality of the use of nuclear weapons by the United States *under certain conditions*, the chief of which was that the Government must be *morally certain* "that a similar attack is being mounted and [is] ready to be launched against this country from any source...".

Such views[6] coming from a clergyman were unconventional at that time and to some persons they were also provocative. The more commonly heard opinions of clergymen on this issue stressed the immorality of nuclear warfare, whatever the circumstances. And probably a majority of them, in the 1950s, simply evaded this agonizing subject.

But Walsh did not: he addressed it forthrightly. His position on the matter was in accord with the major tenets of his public philosophy throughout three decades: the Soviet Union's ultimate international objective was world domination, and the United States must confront and repel Soviet foreign policy by all the requisite economic and military resources available.

Furthermore, Walsh was a nationalist who viewed the American military establishment, and United States rearmament after World War II, not as some necessary evil, but rather as an integral and constructive force to be used in the conduct of the country's foreign policies.

The final two selections in this anthology, grouped by the editor as Part V, "In Honor of Great Men," are representations of Father Walsh's interest in Catholic historical and humanistic studies. Walsh's homily "A Sermon from a Stained Glass Window" focused on the significance of Thomas More's life as "the patron and most shining example for every Catholic layman." The central message in this tribute to Saint Thomas More concerns the moral obligations of Catholics who hold public office.

Father Walsh's biographical tribute to Gaston, the second selection in Part V, was delivered at the time of Georgetown's own sesquicentennial celebration, during 1938-1939, which coincided with the sesquicentennial of the United States Constitution. These sesquicentennial themes, referred to by Walsh in his 1938 address, take on renewed meaning fifty years later as Georgetown celebrates its own Bicentennial as well as that of the United States Constitution.

For almost a century all members of the Georgetown community have been personally familiar with the intimate, ornate, and graceful auditorium in the University's Healy Building known as Gaston Hall. Father Walsh gave hundreds of public addresses and lectures in the hall. Probably most of the Georgetown community know that it was named after Georgetown's first student, William Gaston. But it is likely that few know much about the life, achievements or significance of the remarkable North Carolinian who remained throughout his life a loyal son of Georgetown.

William Gaston was not merely some parochial figure in Georgetown's history. On the contrary, he enjoyed a distinguished political and legal career both in North Carolina and the national legislature. His achievements were widely recognized during his life: The University of Pennsylvania, Columbia, Harvard, and Princeton, where he graduated, conferred honorary degrees on him. Gaston, a Catholic in a predominantly Protestant society, exemplified in an impressive manner the Georgetown tradition of preparing Catholic men and women for public service in American society.

To those readers who may have had the pleasure of hearing Father Walsh speak at some time in their lives—on the Georgetown campus, in Constitution Hall, or in some of the many lecture halls around the country in which he lectured—these selections will bring back old but fond memories of this most remarkable man. What cannot be conveyed in these pages, unfortunately, is the almost unrivalled eloquence with which Father Walsh delivered all of his addresses and lectures. Nevertheless, this volume will remind all members of the ever expanding community of the Edmund A. Walsh School of Foreign Service of the extraordinary diversity of the many interests and achievements of its Founder, as well as of the historical roots of the unique institution which has so enriched their lives.

Walter I. Giles
Associate Professor of Government
Georgetown University

Notes

1. B.S.F.S./M.A., 1943, 1946; Ph.D., 1956, Georgetown University. The writer of this Introduction has been a member of the Georgetown University community for more than half a century since entering the School of Foreign Service as a freshman in 1938, the beginning of Georgetown's Sesquicentennial Year. He has been a member of the University faculty for more than forty years. During the six-year period, 1944-1950, Professor Giles was personal secretary to the Rev. Edmund A. Walsh, S.J., and he remained a close friend and associate of Father Walsh until the latter's death in 1956. The commentary and opinions expressed in this Introduction are those of the writer.

2. The attendance of Father Walsh at an informal dinner in Washington with Senator Joseph McCarthy gave rise to rumors linking Father Walsh with Senator McCarthy's anti-communist campaign. No basis exists for this rumor.

3. The idea for the educational program that subsequently emerged in the form of the School of Foreign Service may have first developed in discussions between Father Creeden and Constantine E. McGuire. McGuire, a consulting expert in international economic affairs, finance, and foreign commercial law, and a man of considerable influence in government, business, diplomatic and church circles, enjoyed a life-long association with Father Walsh. He is credited with playing a major role in the development of the Foreign Service School during its early years. McGuire's personal history, and the role he may have exerted in the School's formative years, are described in an article by the late Carroll Quigley, for many years professor of history in the School of Foreign Service. (See Carroll Quigley, "Constantine McGuire: Man of Mystery," *The Courier*, vol. 14, no. 2, December 1965, pp. 16-21.) Although Father Walsh has long been officially recognized as the founder of the School, this most innovative and experimental educational enterprise could not have gotten underway without his two principal supporters, the President of the University, and the Provincial of the Maryland Province.

4. The only notable exception to this observation is the brief and singular political career of the Rev. Charles E. Coughlin, the celebrated "radio priest" of the Shrine of the Little Flower at Royal Oak, Michigan. But unlike Father Walsh, Coughlin was never a part of mainstream politics in this country; least of all was he an influence within the American political establishment of his times and his somewhat meteoric political career extended for only a few years.

5. The other Jesuits who had official appointments with the School during the Walsh decades served primarily in administrative capacities for short periods of time. While Father Walsh directed the Papal Relief Mission in Russia, Coleman Nevils headed the School of Foreign Service as its Regent. When Walsh was in Germany following World War II, Thomas Murray was the acting head of the School. In 1949, Father Frank Fadner was assigned to the School at Father Walsh's request. Fadner, with Walsh's strong support, had been trained academically to succeed the Regent at some unspecified date as head of the School. In 1950, Father Walsh created the office of Executive Assistant to the Regent for Father Fadner. And in 1955, when Walsh's serious illness indicated little possibility, if any, of recovery, Fadner was appointed Regent of the School, and Walsh was designated Regent Emeritus.

6. Walsh elaborated the themes of his article in his last published book, *Total Empire: The Roots and Progress of World Communism* (1951). See chap. XI, "Atom Bombs and the Christian Conscience."

PART I:

RUSSIA

As director general of the Papal Relief Mission to the U.S.S.R., Father E.A. Walsh, S.J. signing documents in Moscow, 1922. Looking on, left to right: Father L.J. Gallagher, S.J.; an interpreter; Father J.S. Farrell, S.J.

1. Sic Transit Gloria Mundi

Father Walsh's first assignment abroad took him to Soviet Russia where, for nearly two years—from March 1922 to November 1923—he served by appointment of Pope Pius XI as director general of the Papal Relief Mission and as Vatican representative. During the ensuing four years he traveled widely throughout Europe, gathering firsthand information and background material on the Russian Revolution and its aftermath.

As to the origin of his first book *The Fall of the Russian Empire*, Father Walsh noted that it was "a collateral consequence of a weekend I spent in 1926/27 at Tyringham, in the Berkshires." Mr. Ellery Sedgwick, then editor of the *Atlantic Monthly*, was among the guests. As Father Walsh had recently returned from the Soviet Union, he was asked to talk about his experiences there. This brought him an offer from the editor to put his talk in printed form for the pages of the magazine (January, February and March 1928 issues) and, subsequently, as a full-length volume. Father Walsh believed that the Romanov dynasty ascended to the Russian throne amid chaos and social disruption, not unlike the conditions prevailing when the dynasty fell in 1917, about three hundred years later. For nearly thirty years after the assassination of Ivan the Terrible in 1584—years which were wrought with political strife, confusion and violence—Russia sought a competent ruler and tried to chart her future political life, finally electing Michael Romanov czar in 1613. But during their 304-year reign, the Romanovs often brought Russia to the crossroads of decision and led her on the wrong path in her journey, in the view of Father Walsh. He believed that Peter the Great, the reformist czar, sent Russia furthest along the false path of a spurious European culture that was poorly adapted to her Slavic soul. Successive czars continued this trend, particularly Catherine the Great, the "philosophe on the throne," with her admiration of French intellectual achievements.

The burning of Moscow by the Russians themselves, during the Napoleonic invasion of 1812, was an expression of the Muscovite hatred of Europe, which led them to prefer burning at the stake to another dose of French culture. But the westernizing trend also introduced ideas, such as the notions of security and respect for the individual and social justice, which were of particular interest to educated Russians. Some of them had received a cosmopolitan education abroad and felt estranged from their autocratic government, the Orthodox Church and the common people, and disapproved of keeping the peasants enslaved in legalized bondage. Secret societies flourished and led to a conspiracy to overthrow the government.

In December 1825, upon the death of Alexander I, discontented noblemen and idealistic young officers of the Imperial army led an open revolt in St. Petersburg to end the tyranny of czardom. This was the first appearance of revolutionary force in Russia inspired by an ideological program. But due to the participants' indecision and lack of organization, the uprising was easily thwarted. However, its immediate effect was increased repression under the despotic autocracy of Nicholas I.

The defeat of Russia in the Crimean War encouraged Czar Alexander II to introduce a number of internal reforms, including the reorganization of the army and of the government administration. But the implementation of his crowning achievement, the emancipation of the serfs in 1861, was frustrated by the failure of the ruling classes to relinquish their vested interests. Although politically emancipated, the great masses of the peasantry remained, in effect, economic serfs, and the struggle between the people and the ruling autocracy continued. Frequent agrarian riots, revolts by university students guided by professional agitators from abroad, assassinations of high public officials due to governmental repression, and dissatisfaction of workers united all revolutionary elements into one common cause, the destruction of the old order. Alexander II paid for his enlightened and well-meaning efforts with his life.

Alexander III, ascending the throne after his father's assassination by terrorists, was determined to eradicate revolutionism and reasserted autocracy. He restored Russia's international prestige and promoted industrialization with European capital and technical expertise, while the growing industrial working class was suffering both physical and moral privations.

The events of "Bloody Sunday" in 1905, followed by strikes, demonstrations, peasant insurrections, mutinies of the army and navy, and Russia's humiliating defeat in the war with Japan, appreciably added to political discontent. But weak, irresolute Czar Nicholas II, surrounded by bureaucrats and flatterers, ignored urgent demands by friends and relatives for the creation of a representative government in which people would have confidence. The preconditions for a violent revolt of the oppressed masses against their rulers were thus established and it was only a question of time before the actual hostilities would erupt.

In *The Fall of the Russian Empire* Father Walsh analyzes the events culminating in the Revolution of 1917 and leading to the massacre of the Romanovs, and examines the establishment of the provisional government as well as the advent of bolshevism. The book was well received: "...Never before has the story of the Russian drama been told with such deep insight into its complexity...," wrote the reviewer in the *Independent* of June 23, 1928. "He paints the central figures as Aeschylus or Sophocles might paint them: victims of Nemesis's inexorable fate. And he has something of Dante's vision of Destiny as the revelation of Moral Law...," said the *New York Times Book Review* of July 1, 1928.

The following chapters from the book describe the last days of the Romanovs.

Chapter X

The House of Special Designation

On May 23 the Tzarevitch Alexis and his three sisters arrived at Ekaterinburg from Tobolsk; the entire family was thus reunited, never again to be separated. But the two foreign tutors, Gilliard and Gibbs, were not permitted to continue in attendance on their pupils. They remained in Ekaterinburg, however, until the arrival of the White troops.

The imprisonment which now began was far different in character and severity from the preceding periods. Brutality replaced respect, and the thirst for vengeance became increasingly apparent in the attitude of the jailers. Two hoardings of rough logs and planks were erected around the Ipatiev house, the outer one a short distance from the first stockade, leaving a walking space between. These barricades reached to the level of the second-story window-tops, thus completely isolating the prisoners from sight and the outside world from them. To ensure a complete screen, the windows themselves were painted. The Grand Duchess Anastasia, driven desperate by the isolation, once opened her window and looked out. She was driven back by a shot from a sentry, the bullet lodging in the woodwork of the window frame. A machine gun was mounted on the roof of the house directly opposite and trained on the Ipatiev house; guards were

---

Chapters X and XI from *The Fall of the Russian Empire—The Story of the Last of the Romanovs and the Coming of the Bolsheviki*, by Edmund A. Walsh, S.J. Published by Little, Brown, and Company, Boston, 1928. Reprinted by permission.

posted at every corner of the stockade as well as at the doors of the rooms where the prisoners ate, slept, and congregated. The first floor was occupied by the Bolshevist guards; the royal family was quartered on the second.

For the first time the prisoners were subjected to personal search. Avdeiev, the Commandant of the "House of Special Designation," rudely snatched a reticule from the hands of the Empress. Nicholas protested: "Until now I have had honest and respectful men around me."

Didkovsky, one of the searchers, retorted: "Please remember that you are under arrest and in the hands of justice."

Tchemodourov, the Tzar's faithful valet who accompanied the family throughout their imprisonment, has left, under oath, a deposition the bare recital of which makes comment superfluous:

> Night and day three Red guards were posted on the first floor, one at the door, one in the vestibule, and one at the door of the [only] toilet. The conduct of these men was gross; cigarettes hanging on their lips, vulgar and half-clothed, their looks, actions, and habitual manners inspired fear and disgust.... When the young Grand Duchesses passed on their way to the toilet room the guards followed, under pretense of watching them; they addressed indecent remarks to the girls, asking them whither they were going and for what purpose. While the girls were inside the guards lounged against the door.... The food was bad, coming all prepared from a Soviet dining room. [Later they were allowed to have their own cook.] Their Majesties always ate in company with the domestics... They would put a soup tureen on the table, but there would not be enough spoons or knives or forks. The Red guards sat by our side and ate from the same dishes. One day a soldier plunged his spoon into the soup tureen, saying, "Enough for you—I will be served." Another day Avdeiev [the Commandant] kept his hat on and smoked a cigarette. As we ate our cutlets, he took his plate and,

interposing his arms between the Emperor and the Empress, helped himself. As he took the meat, he managed to bend his elbow and strike the Emperor on the chin.

The very walls of the Ipatiev house, particularly in the lavatory, were made to contribute something to the mental suffering of the helpless victims. The guards, under the tutelage of a certain Bielomoine, covered them with ribald verses and gross sketches caricaturing the Empress and Rasputin. On another occasion Faya Safonov, one of the most offensive of the guard, climbed a fence to the level of the Tzarina's window and sang filthy songs at her.

The girls had a swing in the garden; the soldiers carved indecent words on the seat. Under the moral torture and physical confinement—toward the end the prisoners were allowed but five minutes in the garden each day—the ex-Tzar maintained that astonishing external calm and passivity which characterized his whole life. His health did not seem to weaken, nor did his hair whiten. During the few minutes allowed for exercise in the open air, he carried the Tzarevitch in his arms, as the boy was unable to walk, and marched stolidly up and down until his precious five minutes were over. But the Empress never left the porch; she aged visibly, her health failed, and gray hairs appeared.

The first days of July brought important and ominous changes in the personnel guarding the prisoners. Avdeiev, together with his colleagues, Moshkin and all the peasant-soldiers who had been recruited locally from the Zlokazov and Sissert factories, were dismissed or removed to a position outside the house. All "key" stations were taken by "reliable" guards, a sure indication that murder was contemplated. Three entirely new figures glide into the picture—Jankel Mikhailovich Jurovsky, who assumed the duties of Commandant vacated by Avdeiev, Chaia Isaacovich Golostchekin, an active and influential member of the Bolshevist Party, and Alexander Georgevich Bieloborodov, the twenty-five-year-old peasant who served as President of the Soviet of the Ural region. ...All three were leading spirits in the local organ of terrorism, the *Chrezvychaika*, commonly called the "Cheka" or secret police, and had contributed their share to its final roll call of 1,800,000 victims. All, particularly Golostchekin, were in close relation with...Jankel Sverdlov, who was, at that time, undisputed master of Moscow as Chairman of the Central Executive Committee of the All-Russian Congress. It was to Sverdlov that reports would be directed from Ekaterinburg.

The new arrivals were accompanied by ten Lettish soldiers—that is, by a detachment of those hardened shock troops whose ruthless brutality won for them the reputation of being the bashibazouks of the Russian Revolution. In the present case certain circumstances would indicate that this group were really Magyars. In any case, the Cheka simply followed its common practice in thus removing all strictly Russian guards from immediate participation in the most comprehensive act of regicide in the history of a people whose annals reek with deeds of violence and bloodshed.

Golostchekin had been in Moscow for the two weeks preceding the night of the murder, remaining absent until the fourteenth of July. During that time he was closeted in frequent conference with Sverdlov, with whom he lodged. Bieloborodov kept him informed by wire of events at the Ipatiev house. Thus in early July, the following telegram was dispatched:

Moscow. Sverdlov for Golostchekin.... Jurovsky replaces Avdeiev. The indoor guard has been entirely changed.

BIELOBORODOV

In the meantime, Jurovsky had been seen by townsfolk on several occasions surveying the woods in the suburbs of Ekaterinburg; a week before the murder he was discovered in the same occupation near the locality which subsequent investigation determined as the spot where the funeral pyre had been erected.

On July 14, the day of Golostchekin's return from Moscow, an Orthodox priest of Ekaterinburg, Storojev by name, was permitted to celebrate Mass for the prisoners. He testified later that Jurovsky had remarked:

"You have said Mass here before?"
"Yes."
"Well and good. You will do it once again."

Storojev further deposed:

According to the liturgy governing a low Mass, at a determined moment the following prayer must be read: "May the souls of the departed rest in peace with Thy saints." I do not know why he did it, but my deacon, instead of merely reading the prayer, began to chant it. [This prayer is never *sung* except at funerals.] I followed suit, though somewhat irritated at his violation of the canons. We had barely begun when we heard, behind us, the noise of the whole imperial family throwing themselves on their knees.... At the end of the service they all approached to kiss the Cross and the deacon gave the Blessed Bread to both Emperor and Empress.... The deacon and I left in silence.... Suddenly, in front of the School of Fine Arts, the deacon said to me, "Do you know, something has happened to them." As his words corresponded exactly to what I was thinking, I stopped and asked him why he thought so. "I am sure," he said; "they seem so changed, and not one of them sang today." He was right, because for the first time, on July 14, not one of the Romanovs accompanied us by singing.

On Monday, the fifteenth, four women were admitted into the death house and ordered to scrub the parquet floors. Their testimony, taken before the Commission of Inquiry, establishes the fact that the entire imperial family was alive on that day and in good health. On the same day, two lay sisters from a local institution, Antonina Trinkina and Maria Krokhaleva, presented themselves as usual with milk for the prisoners. Jurovsky himself received the charitable offering and informed them that on the morrow, July 16, they should bring not only milk but fifty eggs, carefully packed in a basket. This the good Samaritans gladly did on the sixteenth, all unconscious of the cynical preparation Jurovsky was making to ensure a luncheon for his executioners in the woods after the deed of blood was done and the traces removed. During the minute examination of the ground in the forest at the spot where the bodies were cremated, the indefatigable Nicholas Sokolov discovered a mass of broken eggshells.

Final preparations seem to have been completed by Tuesday, July 16. On that day the boy Leonid Sednev, a playmate of the Tzarevitch, was removed from the house and transferred to an adjoining building. He was never seen again, except for a brief moment next day as he sat in tears at an open window. Five motor lorries were requisitioned from the official Bolshevist garage and the chauffeurs were instructed to have them in readiness outside the Ipatiev house at midnight. On one of these trucks were placed two barrels of benzine and a few smaller jugs containing a supply of sulphuric acid. The Commission of Inquiry which gathered and laboriously analyzed every scrap of evidence bearing on the gruesome happenings of those twenty-four hours was able to establish, from the confiscated receipts delivered by Jurovsky for these supplies, that the barrels held more than three hundred litres of benzine and the jugs one hundred and ninety kilogrammes of the deadly acid. These destructive precautions had been obtained on mandates signed by Voikov, who paid for his zeal with his life; he was assassinated by a Russian exile at Warsaw, in June 1927.

The instruments of death were provided; the grave was ready; the executioners were resolved, and the victims were asleep in their beds. It was Tuesday night, July 16, 1918.

Chapter XI

The Tragedy Ends

The knell sounded shortly after midnight, when Jurovsky knocked at the door of the ex-Emperor and bade Nicholas arise and dress. The same summons was delivered to the Tzarina, the children, and their suite. Jurovsky explained to Nicholas that the Siberian army, under Admiral Kolchak, and the Czechoslovak troops, those former prisoners of war who had succeeded in arming themselves and were now a serious menace to the Soviet régime in Siberia, were approaching Ekaterinburg; an engagement was imminent, and bullets would be flying in the streets. In his solicitude for the safety of the royal family he must insist that they come below stairs, where they would be secure from accident or injury.

The ex-Tzar, seemingly, was satisfied, credulous as always, and did not appear to suspect a trap. The women dressed and washed, not omitting, however, to put on the specially prepared clothes into the lining and hems of which they had previously sewn jewels and bank notes against the hoped-for day of escape. Several cushions had likewise been filled with precious stones and money; in all, one million rubles, something over $500,000, had been secreted in this manner.

To reach the safe place designated by Jurovsky, they descended a flight of steps, passed into the open courtyard, and thence approached a semibasement, eighteen by sixteen feet in dimensions. The single door was open, awaiting their coming; there was no other exit, as the inside door entering into a second room was barred and obstructed on the far side. The only window, opening on to the Vosnesensky Lane that skirted the side of the house, was protected by a heavy iron grille. Outside this window stood sentries, their faces pressed against the grimy glass, able to see all that passed within, especially as the room had been lighted for the better aim of the executioners. The testimony of these onlookers forms one of the strongest elements in the convincing depositions gathered during the inquiry.

There was, moreover, another window, opening not directly into the room, but into a lobby before it; this window commanded a view of the interior, and here too stood a sentry who witnessed the butchery. The deposition of Medvedev, one of the actual participants in the murder, later captured by the Whites; the description given to Yakimov by Klescheev and Deriabin, the sentries who gazed spellbound through these windows; and the account of Proskouriakov, the Red Guard who removed the bloodstains from the floor with water, mop, and sawdust, make it possible to reconstruct the tragedy in all its hideous detail.

The midnight procession, in passing through the dim courtyard, must have seen the motor trucks silhouetted against the summer sky. In that northern latitude it is light until after 10 P.M.; it is never wholly dark, especially on clear nights, and dawn appears as early as two in the morning. They doubtless imagined the vehicles were for their escape in case of danger, or possibly for the baggage. Not one of the victims seems to have suspected what lay beyond that open door through which light was streaming into the courtyard. Above, nothing to be seen but sharp points of light, like a myriad watching eyes in a clear blue sky; below, shadowy figures lurking at corners and along the inner stockade; no sound, except the shuffling of many feet on the dirt walk. Jurovsky marshaled them, leading the way and beckoning toward the open door; behind followed Medvedev and the scowling Letts, eleven men, fingering their pistols as they closed in on their unsuspecting victims....

Once having entered, exit for them is barred by the executioners, who mass themselves before the door, awaiting the prearranged signal. Nicholas, still believing that the family is about to be conveyed to a place of safety, requests that chairs be brought for the Empress and the children. It is done. They rest, waiting in simple expectation, hats on and clad in traveling clothes.

At this point the available testimony, which covers volumes, diverges slightly, but only in unimportant chronological details. According to some witnesses, Jurovsky, standing at the head of his file, suddenly produced a paper and read what purported to be a death warrant which authorized him to execute "Nicholas the Bloody and all his family"; others, not mentioning the death warrant, depose that Jurovsky suddenly addressed Nicholas and said: "Your relatives have sought to rescue you, but it could not be managed by them and so we ourselves are obliged to kill you."

The ex-Tzar did not seem to understand and asked: "What do you mean?"

"This is what I mean!" cried Jurovsky, firing point-blank at the Emperor with his automatic revolver, killing him instantly.

The scene that followed must await its own proper Dante. Twelve revolvers bellowed thunder and spat tongues of fire; the hollow chamber, reverberating with the explosions, filled up with smoke and acrid fumes; not once nor twice, but again and again each Lett, frenzied with primeval bloodlust, fired, choosing his own particular victim. With twelve men letting loose the pent-up hatreds of three hundred years, it is not unreasonable to expect that each emptied the clip of his automatic, which would make nearly a hundred shots. Medvedev, a participant, confessed that the sight, with the blended smell of blood and powder fumes, nauseated him. The petrified onlookers at the windows were harrowed by the shrieks of women and the groans of men; Alexis, the Tzarevitch, was not killed outright, but moaned and writhed over the bodies of his dead parents. It was Jurovsky who finally dispatched him with his revolver. Those who still breathed were bayoneted to death. The floor was chipped and torn with bayonet thrusts driven through the soft bodies. A little dog, a King Charles spaniel, pet of the Grand Duchess Anastasia and brought down by her in her arms, ran hysterically about, darting between the legs of friend and foe, barking furiously. Floor and walls were spattered with blood and bits of clinging flesh.

Twenty-three living persons had entered that narrow cellar—eleven prisoners and the twelve guards conducting them to a place of greater safety. As dawn began to streak the sky, twelve persons came out, leaving eleven corpses safely within, lying in pools of blood that trickled in widening circles out into the corridor. Such evidence must be removed; Jurovsky called for Proskouriakov to mop up the floor, scatter sawdust about, and cleanse the walls. Sheets were then brought from upstairs; into them the bleeding bodies were rolled and then piled pell-mell into the waiting motor truck, precedence no longer observed.

Twelve miles northwest of Ekaterinburg, on the shores of Lake Isset, stands the secluded little village of Koptiaki in the centre of a heavily wooded forest. Once the site of extensive mining operations, it was now deserted, save for the scattered peasant families who remained unaffected by the coming and going of miners and engineers. Off the beaten track, forgotten and insignificant, the Siberian hamlet slumbered in obscurity—until July 17, 1918.

Early that morning, Anastasia Zykova, a peasant, accompanied by her son Nicholas and her daughter-in-law Maria, started before sunup for Ekaterinburg, with horse and cart, to sell their catch of fish. They had barely passed one of the abandoned mines—the one known as "Four Brothers" because of the four pine trees that once stood there—when they perceived a procession of some sort approaching them. It took the form of several vehicles guarded by Red horsemen. Barely recovered from their surprise at the early morning apparition, they were further dismayed when two of the horsemen galloped swiftly forward to intercept them. The soldiers reined up before the Zykovi, ordered them curtly and with menace in their voices to turn back to their village, and, above all, not to dare to look behind. The simple peasants obeyed, turned their horse's head toward home, and retreated. But one of the women looked back, whereupon the two Red Guards galloped in pursuit and with drawn revolvers accompanied the party nearly a mile, threatening them with instant death if they attempted to see what was going on behind them.

In a short time the village of Koptiaki was buzzing with excitement. Men crept out on all fours across the fields in the direction taken by the motor truck and carts of the cortège; the tracks led across open ground toward one of the shafts of the old Isetsky mine. But the village scouts found that sentries had been stationed in a wide circle, completely isolating the locality; frightened and wondering, they crawled back and awaited developments. Toward evening they saw in the heavens glowing reflections from a great bonfire kindled on the spot where the Bolsheviki had finally halted. The hidden rite, whatever it was, continued throughout the next day; only on Thursday, July 19, were the woods deserted and silent.

Then, and only then, did a group of peasants venture to approach the scene. They found the space around the shaft littered with débris of various kinds—disturbed foliage, remnants of a fire, charred wood, and piles of ashes. But on poking under the ashes with sticks they encountered a collection of burnt objects that gave rise to horrible suspicions: first, a Maltese cross set with emeralds, six corset steels from women's corsets, a miscellaneous collection of charred buttons, buckles, parts of slippers, hooks and eyes, beads, parts of women's clothing, and a number of small, dirty pebbles which, on being cleaned and treated chemically, turned out to be pure diamonds. Francis McCullagh, that brilliant and supremely daring journalist who visited these scenes a few weeks after the murder and interrogated the peasants and even Jurovsky himself, spent many weeks—trying weeks—with the present writer in Moscow. He recounted his findings at Ekaterinburg in considerable detail. It was the discovery of that Maltese cross that led to the ghastly truth. Such a decoration was worn only by personages high in the Imperial Service. Pometkovsky, one of the searchers, who was in reality an escaped royalist officer in hiding, knew that there was but one such person in Ekaterinburg. As other metallic and stone objects that had resisted the fire but plainly revealed their late owners were placed before him, he cried aloud: "God Almighty! Can they have burned the whole family alive?"

He was right, but not entirely so; they had burned them, but not while alive.

The spot for the cremation of the bodies had been chosen in advance by Jurovsky and extraordinary precautions taken to destroy the *corpus delicti*. Subsequent events, however, have proved that, though the bodies of the victims can never be produced as primary evidence of the crime, the boast of Voikov, "The world will never know what we have done with them," has not been justified. The elaborate technique of concealment overshot its mark and ignored a number of obvious possibilities. Jurovsky had added to his staff two new assistants whose particular function seems to have been to dismember the bodies. Arrived at the pit, which was thirty feet deep, the regicides set to work to finish their gruesome task. The corpses were drenched with benzine, the countenances having probably first been destroyed by the sulphuric acid, and the human bonfire was then ignited. Acid was likewise used to dissolve the larger and tougher bones which were likely to resist the flames. When fire had consumed all the flesh and reduced skulls and skeletons to ashes, the débris was swept up and cast into the yawning mouth of the iron pit. An attempt was made to rearrange the scarred face of nature by scattering the embers and foliage carelessly about, so as to simulate the appearance of an ordinary camping ground or picnic place. But the wound was too deep; the executioners were tired and probably hurried. They sat down at last beneath the pine trees to eat their lunch, letting fall the telltale eggshells.

The Commission of Inquiry found hundreds of clues and articles definitely identified as belonging to the imperial family: the six sets of corset steels, exactly the number for six women; precious stones in great numbers; the belt buckles of both Tzar and Tzarevitch; the buckles of the women's shoes; hooks and eyes and other metallic parts of feminine wear; the broken lense of the Empress's eyeglasses; a set of artificial teeth identified as those of Dr. Botkin; fragments of chopped and sawed human bones; and one human finger, long, slender, well-shaped, probably cut from the Empress's hand to get at a ring. This pathetic collection of relics, the meagre débris of a fallen dynasty, this admixture of human bones and ashes, corset steels and diamond dust, was transported in a single trunk to Harbin and from thence to "a sure place." That is all the record shows; where or how far they wandered after crossing into Mongolia I know not.

So passed Nicholas II and the Romanovs, to be followed by a third Nicholas, called Lenin, and the House of the Soviets.

Eight days after these events, on July 25, 1918, Ekaterinburg was evacuated by the Bolsheviki, and the combined Kolchak and Czechoslovak troops entered the city. Five days later, on July 30, an orderly investigation, conducted in a scientific and judicial spirit, was instituted, first under the direction of Judge Nametkin, of that territorial jurisdiction, but later—and fortunately—committed to the very capable hands of Judge Nicholas Sokolov of the Omsk Tribunal. On the evacuation of the town by the Bolsheviki, someone had the presence of mind to rush to the telegraph office and secure possession of the official telegrams that passed between Moscow and the Ural capital during those eventful days; from these records, fortified by the sworn statements of the scores of witnesses and the mute testimony of the hundreds of recognizable clues that had been trampled into the clay in the forest or found at the bottom of the shaft, Sokolov was enabled to publish to an expectant world in 1925 his precious report of 295 pages, totaling 120,000 words. With infinite difficulty, patience, and hazard, he managed to smuggle his material out of Russia to Western Europe, where in peace and safety he edited and published his findings. His work done, he died of hardship and exhaustion.

These documents, of inestimable importance for students of the Russian Revolution, are a monument to the painstaking judicial mind of their author. They set at rest, definitely, all doubts as to the fate of the Romanovs, not only with respect to the immediate family of the Tzar, but also of his near relatives, the grand dukes and princes who were murdered about the same time, either at Petrograd or in the environs of Perm. The murders at Alapaevsk, near Perm, bear a striking resemblance to the Ekaterinburg tragedy. Twenty-four hours after the death of Nicholas, six other Romanovs were officially murdered in that city by the Bolsheviki, their bodies thrown down the shaft of an unused mine, and hand grenades dropped down to ensure complete destruction of life. But the bodies of the Perm victims were eventually recovered and identified.

The moral responsibility for the wholesale butchery of the imperial family would now seem to rest fairly and squarely on the shoulders of the Soviet Government, and can no longer be charged off to an alleged uncontrollable fanaticism on the part of the local Ekaterinburg authorities. It was decided upon, approved, and arranged by Jankel Sverdlov at Moscow; Bieloborodov, Golostchekin, and Jurovsky were merely the executors—most willing executors—of a matured governmental policy. To be sure, contrary protestations have been made and pretexts advanced as fictitious as the inhuman charge of incest brought against Marie Antoinette by Hébert during her trial. But, in the copious light shed upon events by the official telegrams confiscated at Ekaterinburg, such evasion is no longer tenable.

There was but one telegram sent by the Ekaterinburg "Cheka" to Moscow on July 17, the day following the murder; it was signed by Bieloborodov, President of the Ural Soviet. Written in code, the combinations of numbers defied the best cypher experts in Europe for two years. But when human ingenuity had unraveled what other human ingenuity had contrived, the cryptic groupings of numbers fell into the following indictment of Moscow as having had a clear understanding with Ekaterinburg before the murder:

To Moscow, Kremlin, for Gorbounov, Secretary of Council of People's Commissars

<u>Please confirm receipt</u>

Tell Sverdlov that the entire family has met the same fate as its head. Officially, they will perish during the evacuation.

BIELOBORODOV

On the following day, July 18, Sverdlov announced to the Central Executive Committee at Moscow that the Tzar had been killed, adding—falsely—that the remaining members of his family had been moved to a safe place. He knew, by prearranged convention, the exact meaning of the sentence "the whole family has met the same fate as its head." Two days later he gives Golostchekin assurance by telegraph that the Central Government approves the execution and authorizes his friend to publish these facts in Ekaterinburg. On the evening of the twentieth, in a meeting of the regional Soviet of the Urals, public announcement was made of the execution to its members—who were supposed to have ordered the deed on their own initiative. On the following day placards were posted throughout the town informing the inhabitants of the Tzar's death and repeating the falsehood concerning the rest of the family. Every single step was ordered, controlled, and approved from Moscow, by Jankel Sverdlov and his colleagues of the Central Executive Committee.

2. Soviet Russia and the Peace of Europe

At the beginning of 1944, as the defeat of Germany and Japan was becoming more and more assured, Soviet Russia, one of the Allies since Hitler's invasion of her territory in June 1941, was already engaged in creating a new empire, a Pan-Slavic Confederation under communist auspices. Notwithstanding the Soviet Union's declaration to abstain from concluding any separate armistice and her pledges for cooperation and consultations in settling boundaries after the war at international conferences, she followed a unilateral course in defining her claims after an Allied victory. In addition to dominating the adjacent territories, the Soviets attempted to attract, cultivate, and use certain powerful German factions as an opening wedge for the dissemination of communist doctrine in a demoralized, wartorn Germany. Moreover, the Kremlin was pursuing these objectives in a manner that seriously jeopardized the basis for Allied unity.

Father Walsh expressed his concern about Soviet Russia's increasing political influence in Europe and cautioned against becoming complacent about the military alliance between the Soviet Union and the Western democracies against the common Nazi enemy.

In the year 1904, a distinguished British geographer, Sir Halford J. Mackinder, delivered an extraordinarily thoughtful lecture before the Royal Geographical Society at London. In the course of the evening he sketched the influence of geography on the evolution of European civilization and analyzed those material factors such as space, location, natural resources, and immunity from attack by sea which had contributed to the rise of great and powerful states from remote times down to his own day. After citing the historical facts and reviewing the human forces which flowed back and forth across Europe in the agelong quest for power, Sir Halford concluded that the pivot, the central point around which so much world history had been concentrated, was located in that portion of Eurasia which stretches from the Volga to the Yangtze and from the Himalayas to the Arctic Ocean. ...The oversetting of the balance of power in favour of the pivot state, resulting in its expansion over the marginal lands of Euro-Asia, would permit of the use of vast continental resources for fleet-building, and the empire of the world would then be in sight. This might happen if Germany were to ally herself with Russia.

It was there, he declared, on that great tableland unbroken by natural barriers and rich in potential energy that the most important and significant events of history had occurred and it was there, he prophesied, that history would continue to be made.

Again, in 1919, as the victorious Allies gathered at Versailles to remake a shattered Europe, Mackinder returned to

---

Lecture delivered to the League of Catholic Women, at the Hotel Statler, Boston, Massachusetts, on March 19, 1944.

his controlling idea. In a book written for the negotiators of the Treaty and entitled *Democratic Ideals and Realities*, he pointed out certain facts familiar to geographers but neglected by statesmen. This earth of ours is about 3/4 water, with the habitable portion restricted to approximately 1/4 of the surface of the planet. This landmass he conceived as a great island set down in the midst of the overwhelmingly larger body of water. Now, this World Island is composed mainly of the three great continents of the Eastern Hemisphere, Europe, Asia and Africa, with the Western lands, North and South America as well as Australia, considered as minor geographic areas, appendages as it were, when compared with the central mass. That Eastern Hemisphere has, Mackinder again insisted, a central core of historic, economic and military significance which he described in 1919, not as the pivot of history as he had done in 1904, but as the Heartland of the World Island. It coincided roughly with the territory directly controlled by Russia but extending to the areas lying adjacent to the Soviet State.

This conception of global geography can never be accurately demonstrated on a flat map of the world such as the Mercator projection so commonly used in modern times. You must take a globe and study on that true miniature of the earth the relative position of the continents, their sizes, characteristics and juxtapositions. You will then grasp more clearly what Mackinder meant when he summed up his warning in that celebrated passage of his book:

> When our statesmen are in conversation with the defeated enemy, some airy cherub should whisper to them from time to time this saying:
>
> > Who rules East Europe commands the Heartland,
> > Who rules the Heartland commands the World-Island,
> > Who rules the World-Island commands the World.

Finally, in 1943, Mackinder restated his unchanged belief in an article published in the July issue of *Foreign Affairs*.

Everything that has happened in recent years brings confirmation to his theses and now, forty years after his first lecture before the Royal Geographical Society, he repeats his warning:

> "All things considered, the conclusion is unavoidable that if the Soviet Union emerges from this war as conqueror of Germany, she must rank as the greatest land power on the globe. Moreover, she will be the power in the strategically strongest defensive position. The Heartland is the greatest natural fortress on earth. For the first time in history it is manned by a garrision sufficient both in number and quality."

Mackinder's masterful analysis of power politics was not taken seriously in 1904 and 1919, except in one quarter: the German general and geographer, Karl Haushofer, quickly realized its importance and transformed its root principle into the cornerstone of the geopolitics which became a dominating theory in Hitler's Germany and which furnished the geographic argument for the Germanic program of world revolution. From his vantage point as counsellor to Hitler, Haushofer consistently advocated a policy of peace and alliance with Soviet Russia, realizing that between them these two European powers could rule the entire continent and eventually control the world.

His lifelong ambition reached its zenith of fulfillment in the Russo-German Non-Aggression Pact of August 1939, which, when consummated, brought together in active coalition the most formidable military machine in the world and the most inexhaustible source of manpower in Europe.

That agreement and its military consequences marked the greatest menace to western civilization and brought the darkest hour to Christendom since the Mohammedan invasion of Europe. But Hitler's personal "intuition" prevailed over his teacher of geography and over his military advisors as well, with the result that Russia was attacked by her *quondam* ally in a reversal of policy which historians will probably recognize as the point when Hitler himself tipped the scales of destiny in the direction of ultimate defeat. The sequel is current history and this audience needs no recital of the military phases since Stalingrad. But there is much need of facing realistically the political effects of Russia's triumphant march into Western Europe.

During the years of Hitler's campaign to capture the organs of government in Germany, an historic race between two ideologies and two grandiose concepts of power was in progress on the continent of Europe. The spectacular Five-Year Plan of Joseph Stalin was being successfully sold to the Russian Revolution, while a thousand-year vision of Teutonic supremacy was being unfolded to Germans in revolt. Teuton and Slav, historic rivals, were on the march again while England slept, France disintegrated and America grappled with her great depression. Through Lenin's internationalism and Stalin's industrialization, Soviets became the focus of world attention in the first half of the postwar period, while Hitler's success and the challenge of national socialism dominated the second. The Teutonic demands climaxed in 1939 when Hitler's order of the day let loose the dogs of war and affirmed that the destiny of Germany was about to be determined for the next thousand years.

The two concepts, Communism and Nazism, included an identical objective, namely, world revolution. They expressed, each in their own language, the two most dynamic principles, in fact the only dynamic forces, in the European balance of power. By their content and universalism they were inexorably destined for eventual collision. Two such claimants for universal hegemony could not coexist on the same continent and simultaneously activate their programs for a protracted period of time. This was basically clear to both parties long before the German attack on Russia in June, 1941. Both in their own way, accepted the dogma of Hitler formulated in *Mein Kampf*: "Political parties are inclined to compromise; world concepts never. Political parties count on adversaries; world concepts proclaim their infallibility." Both secretly understood the nature of the breathing space afforded by the Russo-German Non-Aggression Pact of August 1939.

Without that indispensable cooperation, Hitler would never, I am confident, have dared to cross the Rubicon of decision on September 1, 1939. Had Russia not remained aloof but mobilized, I do not believe that Germany would ever have invaded Poland. The alliance with Germany enabled Stalin to do two things: prepare militarily for the inevitable struggle between the two titans most concerned with the domination of Mackinder's heartland, and establish immediately, for political purposes, a chain of territorial outposts, by extinguishing the independent republics of Latvia, Estonia and Lithuania, by occupying half of the stricken Poland and by attempting the conquest of Finland.

These were the first maneuvers toward the political objectives which Soviet Russia had consistently pursued since the first shot of World War II was fired. Her subsequent political actions have been called mysterious, unpredictable, devious, disconcerting, unintelligible and generally amazing for a power allied to England and the United States in a joint campaign for collective security. But they are such only to those unable or unwilling to admit certain very simple truths.

Hitler's decision to attack his Muscovite rival on June 22, 1941, abruptly restored the true *status quaestionis* of Central Europe. Russia's amazing resistance simply threw her not so much into the camp of the Allies, as back into her original domestic defensive position regarding Hitler Germany. In step with the logic of events and under pressure of new circumstances, the Kremlin wisely shifted to a less intransigent position respecting world revolution and the status of religion in Russia. By first dissolving the Third International, then welcoming the election of a Patriarch to preside over the Orthodox Church, and finally by scrapping the offensive song, the "Internationale" and substituting a new national anthem in praise of the motherland, the Soviet Union quickly scored three distinct psychological triumphs over Nazi Germany. But it would be premature to conclude that her basic external policy, her geopolitical position had been altered to a corresponding degree.

The world was induced to accept the first gesture as public proof that Moscow's hopes for a communist world revolution had been abandoned. That, I believe, was an erroneous conclusion. What Moscow really abandoned was a crude, boisterous and provocative instrumentality which had not only failed to accomplish its revolutionary objectives, but had proved an embarrassment and a stumbling block in the new partnership which Russia formed after the failure of her association with fascism in 1939. Her pact with Nazi Germany in that year enabled her to occupy by force half of Poland and most of the Baltic States, thereby achieving by one strike what the Comintern had not been able to accomplish in twenty years.

Furthermore, the appearance in Moscow of a Free Polish Committee, a Free German Committee and a Free Austrian Committee, all formed and operating under Soviet auspices, served fair notice that Europe was not to be reconstructed solely from Casablanca, Cairo, Quebec, London and Washington, D.C. Also, once Moscow's concrete interest in the geography of Eastern Europe was involved, her attitude changed and hardened to a degree that has caused deep concern in the United Nations. By categorically stating that she intended to retain certain large areas of Polish territory from which her troops had expelled the Nazi invaders, Russia reverted to the very principle of unilateral action which, the world had been given to understand must disappear from the conduct of international relations. The Moscow and Teheran Conferences had pledged a reconstructed world which would be built on the firm foundation of collective cooperation under law and governed by orderly processes of consultation, but the international community was soon to realize that such was not the case.

When Wendell Wilkie, in a friendly article entitled "Don't Stir Distrust of Russia," ventured to recommend that the Soviets should show liberality and restraint in dealing with Poland and the Baltic States, he was bitterly attacked as a meddler by the authoritative *Pravda*, the official organ of the Russian Communist Party. Two more incidents quickly followed which deepened apprehension in London and Washington, D.C.: the same *Pravda* and the government-controlled radio reported in January of this year a sensational story which charged that British agents had been secretly negotiating with Nazi officials over terms of peace. The insinuation was indignantly denied as an insult by the British press and emphatically repudiated by the British Foreign Office and by Lord Halifax, the British Ambassador in Washington, D.C. Furthermore, Moscow refused to consider the offer of mediation tendered by the Government of the United States with respect to the Polish-Russian controversy.

A very definite pattern is thus observable in the evolution of Russia's foreign policy. Militarily she is following the main objective, shared by all Allies, of defeating the common enemy. Politically, she is following a dual policy, as concluded by Hanson Baldwin, the skilled military analyst of *The New York Times*. Obviously, she is anticipating her Allies by staking out her own claims in the post-war world, while England and America are honorably holding to the agreement that all political questions involving territory and other permanent adjustments should be deferred until military victory has been achieved. As a result, they are subjecting themselves to heavy handicaps which will surely operate to their disadvantage when the final accounting begins.

As the Allied forces approach Rome...the question of a new Italian government looms increasingly larger on the horizon of issues clamoring for immediate attention. By attempting to weaken, through insults in the official government newspaper, *Izvestia*, the moral and spiritual authority of their most hated opponent, the Catholic Church, the Communists hope to eliminate one more obstacle in their road to the seizure of power. In accord with this strategy, the Soviet Government will demand participation in every Allied commission set up to govern occupied territory, while categorically refusing to admit the slightest cooperation of

England or the United States in determining the future of liberated Poland, Latvia, Lithuania and Estonia. It was for that purpose that the new technique of "revolutionary legality" was introduced. By quickly incorporating those occupied territories into the Soviet Union and declaring them integral parts of the Communist State, the Commissars consider the matter closed and a purely internal affair, as it were, which is not open to adjudication by outsiders any more than the status of California under the American Constitution. The principles of the Atlantic Charter and the declarations made at the Moscow and Teheran conferences were inapplicable in the remises and Moscow can thus claim that she is not breaking her plighted word. She takes the stand that the Soviet Union alone is judge of her own actions in Eastern Europe, but that the other contracting parties are bound to admit her to full participation in the reconstruction of Western Europe.

The small nations of the world are particularly concerned over the duel now in progress between the spirit of the Atlantic Charter and the realities developing in Europe. They maintain that strong powers, notably the Soviet Union, will never achieve lasting peace if sheer might prevails over individual right. The Dutch, the Swedes, the Belgians and others are wondering whether it shall become customary for any powerful government to request its weaker neighbor, as Russia has told Poland, to dismiss a particular cabinet if it does not find favor in the eyes of the stronger state. Mr. Stanley Bruce, the Australian High Commissioner, spoke the mind of all small states on January 27, of this year, when he said in London that "the smaller nations will never accept the domination of the great powers."

The Soviet Union is also introducing domestic arrangements in support of her foreign policy. The Moscow authorities recently announced the decentralization of the political machinery of their Government which will put "16 Russias" in the field of international relations where before we saw but one. This extension of sovereignty to each of the constituent republics will provide 15 new instruments of pressure and 15 new units for representation of Russian policy in any world conference dealing with the reconstruction of Europe. By granting greater autonomy, in form at least, to all the federated republics, Moscow will be in position to insist that the recently annexed territories are perfectly satisfied with their new status, a pronouncement one may safely prophesy as the premiers and other high officials will obviously be appointees of the Communist Party. Also, such a coup d'état will have a collateral effect of great importance, as other countries, which in the post-war confusion may be wavering between right, center or left forms of political and social organization, will thus receive a subtle invitation to embrace the Communist solution of their problems. This process will be further helped by the Communist cells within each country and stimulated by a "Free Committee of Exiles" residing in Moscow. At a given moment a leftist government would be proclaimed in the disputed area as representing the true voice of the people and then we would see the 17th constituent republic in an expanding Soviet Empire. A similar procedure will probably be applied to Yugoslavia, Bulgaria, Greece and Romania. The ultimate goal may reasonably be deduced from the fundamental dogmas of Marxism, still controlling the Moscow government and never repudiated.

The resolution of the complicated impasse created by the Soviet Union since the Teheran Conference represents a challenge indeed to American and British statesmanship. But in our response, one extreme in particular should be avoided; many Americans are loathe to discuss this difficulty frankly and sincerely because of the absurd contention that he who criticizes Communism at present is giving aid and solace to Hitler. Even a rigorously documented analysis of Soviet foreign policy, as distinguished from her military effort, will frequently expose the analyst to the accusation of being a Fascist and a wrecker of unity. And the epithet will first be hurled by the very same chameleons who maintained an ignominious silence during the 22 months of the Soviet Union's military partnership with Hitler.

President Roosevelt guardedly admits that he is bewildered, and Secretary of State Hull had to content himself with the frigid formularies of diplomacy when he announced last Friday that Soviet Russia's unilateral actions would in nowise change the policy of the American Government. But the ordinary American citizen finds himself in a cruel quandary: devoting heart, soul and body to the cause of the United Nations, he suddenly experiences a chilling and hostile opposition if he presumes even to question the actions of Mr. Stalin or rate them as anything short of inspired and salvific. Congress may be lampooned and ridiculed, the President calumniated, the American people belittled and their war effort minimized, but Mr. Stalin's demand for a second front must be respected.

The insistent demand that Allied troops hurl themselves at the formidable deathtrap erected by Nazi Germany along the coastline of Western Europe is the only war effort that will satisfy these impatient Hotspurs whose loyalty to America seems measured by the extent to which America serves an alien emergency. A second front is defined according to their wishes, despite the fact that American forces in great numbers have fought heroically in Northern Africa, Sicily, Southern Italy, China, Burma, in skies over Germany, on the Atlantic, and in the waters and on the islands of the Pacific; heroic convoys of the Merchant Marine have nattled their way through the dangers of the Arctic night and the perils of Nazi submarines to land supplies for Russia over the Murmansk route, while others have toiled under the killing heats of tropical suns to carve out a transport route from Basra on the Persian Gulf to the southern borders of Russia in Central Asia.

Cooperation is a two-way street and it is high time that someone in high places should say so. Private comment or even the press will not suffice to meet adequately this crisis in our international relations. Public opinion is beginning to insist on more equitable conduct by Soviet Russia in discharging the high responsibility now devolving on her as well as on the other members of the United Nations. "Russia

Must Choose" is the title of a courageous appeal directed to Moscow by a group of distinguished American citizens, all of whom have been leaders in the campaign to aid the Soviet Union and to favorably interpret her role to our people. If the Soviet Union chose to solve the problem of Poland on a unilateral basis, without mediation of her Allies or consent of the Polish people, she would estrange not only millions of Americans, but also many other nationals in small conquered or satellite countries. The latters' hope for an Allied victory would be dashed if they had to expect the same fate as Poland. As such default would be worth many battalions to Hitler, the writers hoped that the Soviet Union would decide to act in accordance with the agreed principles of the Atlantic Charter.

But other developments make me believe that Soviet Russia has now progressed from a dual political policy to a triple course of conduct. I suggest that the last practice represents a strategy of creating confusion in the minds of her partners in London and Washington, D.C. Her activities in Yugoslavia fall in this third category. Moscow has always supported Tito because she knows him by the name of Broz, a noted Communist whose Yugoslav volunteers fought in the Spanish Civil War. By backing him but by also recognizing the government in exile representing King Peter, Moscow leaves it to the world at large to decide just where her game is leading. In this she has some respectable fellowship, however, as both England and America seem inclined to follow a similar paradoxical procedure.

But in suddenly recognizing Marshal Badoglio's Government as the legitimate mouthpiece of the Italian State and offering to exchange ambasssadors, Moscow threw a veritable bombshell of discord and confusion into the tent of the Allied High Command. Done without any consultation, as Secretary Hull announced [on March 17th], this maneuver runs counter not only to Communist opinion in Italy but also to the desires of groups represented by Count Sforza and other Italian spokesmen who have been clamoring for the abolition of the monarchy which Badoglio supports. In commenting editorially on Moscow's paradoxical support of the Italian monarchy, *The Washington Post* stated that it must be left to crystal gazers to figure that one out. But it needs no clairvoyant to see that a beautiful state of Macchiavellian confusion has been created by another unilateral démarche of our Muscovite brothers-in-arms.

The announcement by President Roosevelt that one-third of the Italian fleet or its equivalent would be turned over to the Soviet Union created consternation both in Italy and in London. Presumably this decision was in reply to pressure from Moscow, as it is inconceivable that the President would have decided to take such a disturbing action. Here again we have another example of Moscow's claims to participate in every aspect of the Western European drama. From England came the prompt declaration that no such distribution of the Italian navy was to be thought of and from Italy evidences of so great resentment, that the good name of the United States has suffered serious damage. The net result has been confusion, misunderstanding and ill-will among friends, all engineered from Moscow.

One thing is certain: we are face to face with stark realities which demand clear thinking and expert diplomacy as well as powerful military assault, as we approach the crisis of the war. Instead of cultivating unity by adherence to the Moscow and Teheran declarations, Soviet Russia has deliberately followed an opposite, unilateral course. Does this mean that the Soviet Union will attempt to impose Communism by force in the peripheral states of Europe? Not necessarily. In the territories directly absorbed into the Soviet Union that will undoubtedly be done, but others will be seduced by invitation, by propaganda and by intrigue of the local Communist bodies. Spheres of influence will be created and protectorates contrived until a far-flung Communist empire will be created. Such domain would stretch from the Arctic Circle to the Black Sea, from Vladivostok to Central Europe, dominate the Balkans and reach the Mediterranean via the Adriatic through Yugoslavia.

This conclusion would seem to be the most rational hypothesis capable of explaining Russia's determination to intervene increasingly in Western Europe and the Near East, while resisting Allied cooperation in Eastern Europe. The only other hypotheses would be the need for providing security against possible attack or for additional territory to meet the pressure of population increase and to promote economic development. This last hypothesis may be summarily dismissed, as no informed human being can see such motivation for a country already embracing approximately one-seventh of the inhabitable area of the earth with huge reserves of sparsely settled land, and being admittedly rich in actual and potential resources. There remains, consequently, only the claim of security against attack from without and the psychological drive to export something from within. Let us examine each of these alternative explanations:

Where an attack upon the Soviet Union would originate is a mystery known only to the planner of their present policy. The one power capable of endangering the Soviet Union's security would be Germany. But this country, by common consent, will be made impotent to do such a thing after the Allied victory. This essential condition for peace in Europe is the one objective on which all are in agreement. Would the Soviet Union's enemy be Finland? The possibility is too grotesque and ridiculous to entertain. The Scandinavian countries? They are all traditionally peace-loving communities and incapable of menacing the Titan of the steppes. Belgium and the Netherlands? Equally fantastic. France, Austria, Italy? The ravages of Nazi occupation, the spoilations and weariness of total exhaustion will preclude any warlike adventure for generations to come. Hungary? Equally out of serious consideration. Only Switzerland, Portugal, Andorra and Monaco remain as possible threats to Soviet security. To name them is to dismiss them from the category of aggressors.

As I already mentioned, Yugoslavia, Bulgaria, Greece and Romania will doubtless be included within the sphere of Soviet influence and no menace exists in those quarters.

Czechoslovakia is already aligned with Soviet Russia and can be counted on to cooperate with Moscow, as indicated in the recent treaty negotiated by Mr. Beneš. In a word, no motive can suffice to explain the Soviet Union's present egocentric and illiberal policy beyond her determination to exercise a gigantic regional influence and create a Pan-Slavic confederation in which the influence of Communist ideology, if not directly imposed on all the units, would nevertheless enjoy free entry and full scope for the dissemination of Marxist materialism, now endowed with new prestige borrowed from the military achievements of the Red Army.

The Soviet Union's magnificent resistance to an unprovoked invasion we salute and have supported to the very limit of human possibility, as the report of the Lend-Lease operations amply confirms. Her concomitant attempt to profit from the present world tragedy and, under cover of the confusion incident to global warfare, to seek first to nullify her plighted word and then plan to expand a way of life hostile to Christianity and Democracy, should be exposed and condemned.

3. Communism and the Soviet Threat to Democracy

"Marshal Stalin's greatest Five-Year Plan began in the spring of 1945 with the launching of planned psychological warfare against the United States.... His foreign policy in particular is publicized as a logical vindication of Russian right against Western wrong, of Soviet peace plans against Western warmongers, of Communist nobility against bourgeois hypocrisy," stated Father Walsh in his 1951 book *Total Empire— The Roots and Progress of World Communism*. By 1947, the personal despotism of Stalin extended beyond the borders of Russia well into the remainder of the European Continent.

Soviet Russia's wartime ally, the United States, had emerged from World War II as a powerful nation, ready to take an active role in world affairs: to create political stability, to ensure the continued existence of democratic institutions, and to render assistance to wartorn nations' reconstruction efforts. Thus, when Great Britain withdrew her assistance to Greece, which was plagued by communist insurgency, and when Turkey came under Soviet pressure for military bases, President Truman, in March, 1947, announced his plan for assistance to any nation that was threatened by armed minorities or outside forces. Two months later, Congress passed a bill granting financial aid to these countries in accordance with the "Truman Doctrine." Realizing the serious economic crisis that faced Western European countries and also the danger that poverty and unemployment might be an easy target for communism, the United States sponsored the economic assistance program proposed by Secretary of State George C. Marshall in June, 1947. Economic assistance was offered to both East and West European states, but after preliminary discussion, the Soviets decided not to participate in the Plan and their satellites followed the same policy.

In the fall of 1947, Moscow established a communist information bureau, COMINFORM, with the declared aim of coordinating European Communist parties. The West, however, perceived this organization as an instrument for further extension of Soviet influence in Europe and for complete subordination of all communist parties to the interests of the Soviet Union.

Although during the war the United States and the Soviet Union were united in their common fight against Hitler and overcame their disagreements, after the end of hostilities their ideological differences proved irreconcilable and drove them apart. Peaceful coexistence between the Eastern communist states and Western democracies was not possible. Already in February, 1946, Stalin proclaimed in an official speech that World War II had been caused by modern capitalism and as long as capitalism continued to exist as a political system, wars would be inevitable. One month later, Winston Churchill stated in Fulton, Missouri, that "an iron curtain has descended across the Continent," dividing the East from the West.

In this dismal climate of cold war, Father Walsh stressed the close connection between internal security under the reign of law and the successful solution of international problems, and called "... for men who walk humbly in the sight of God, but keep their powder dry."

May I, at the outset, express to the authorities of the Federal Bureau of Investigation my deep appreciation and abiding gratitude for the privilege of being with you once again to participate in these significant ceremonies. Since the first class assembled in 1935, we have foregathered at regular intervals to assess frankly and earnestly both the **nature** and **incidence** of crime in this country. The skillful and efficient training in crime detection and crime prevention provided by the Federal Bureau of Investigation during those twelve years ushered in a new era of scientific **technique** and initiated a new and very welcome phase of confident **cooperation** between this federal agency and the local police jurisdictions throughout this land. This unity of common objectives in a Democracy traditionally jealous of local prerogatives is, in my opinion, one of the major social benefits deriving from an enterprise which no longer ranks as an experiment but now merits to be considered a national institution.

Once again, the backwash of a world catastrophe has cast up on the beaches of our social life, the ugly flotsam and jetsam of modern civilization in the form of increased domestic crime, increased violence, increased mass psychosis and of that mounting juvenile delinquency, which, in plain accountancy, is really a consequence of adult irresponsibility. Evil root, bitter fruit! I know that these grave and pressing problems on the domestic front have been amply discussed and treated in the laboratories of the Federal Bureau of

---

Address delivered to the Graduates of the Federal Bureau of Investigation National Police Academy, Washington, D.C., on October 3, 1947.

Investigation during your training period and I shall not presume on this occasion to labor the obvious. But, what is extremely important is the relationship which exists between this internal menace and the ever mounting tension in the field of international polity. The security of America begins in the homes of America, on the streets of America, in the stability of our social institutions and on the highways and byways of our economic landscape. These are the anchors and the bedrock of national power. Hence, he who stands watch over these primary safeguards of national security is as much committed to the perpetual vigilance as is the American sentinel at his post of combat on those forward lines of central Europe and the Far East where the peace of the world hangs today balanced on a razor's edge, at the mercy of some deliberate provocation or border incident.

Your task of assuring the reign of law internally is immeasurably complicated by two elements; one is intrinsic to a democracy, while the other arises from a manufactured crisis affecting all humanity. To restore the economic and moral equilibrium of any single participant in a world war of such devastating consequences would, of itself, have been a gigantic task; but to accomplish it in the present mounting demoralization of the entire international community has created a challenge which will require every ounce of our intelligence, our material resources and strength of will.

I have suggested that one of your problems arises from the very nature of the political and social organization traditional in this country. Democracy, though the easiest form of government to establish, since it corresponds most nearly to the heart's desire, is the hardest to maintain. Because of the very generosity of its premise and the universality of its dogmas, it admits to the franchises of freedom every human being possessed of a minimum set of qualifications. Now, there is no more heady wine than freedom recklessly embraced, uncontrolled by discipline, and careless of social responsibility. Hence resulted the appalling crime statistics which you and I have studied with growing concern. Because we revere the dignity of human personality and respect the inalienable rights of individuals to free movement, freedom of expression, free enterprise, to a minimum of police supervision and a maximum of legal protection, we have provided a veritable paradise of opportunity for the evil-minded criminal in this country, for the shyster lawyer and for the racketeers who operate either from the end of a sawed-off shotgun or with smooth legal advice emanating from plushy suites at respectable Fifth Avenue addresses.

These, in part, are the domestic enemies of Democracy, the parasites and moral leeches who abuse the hospitality of our body politic. To thwart them by forehanded vigilance, to apprehend and punish them by just laws and to protect the citizenry of the land against their criminality is the high mission committed to your hands. But the axe must be laid to the roots of motivation and to prevention as well as to the flower and fruit of vicious conduct. The police function will be limited to a sterile and frustrated repetition of routine arrests until the public conscience responds to the dictates of its collective responsibility.

There is an hour for greatness in the lives of nations as well as in the fortunes of individuals. The American people, in the 170 years of their national existence, have achieved a measure of material strength, industrial efficiency, financial opulence and inventive genius which, when aroused and mobilized to indignation, came twice in twenty-five years to the rescue of the parent European civilization. In the field of physical prowess, material resources, organizational aptitude and ability to use force when needed, the democracy of the United States will never again be lightly challenged by any power on the face of the earth. The last word in the science of warfare, the Prussian military caste freely acknowledge by the lips of Field Marshall von Rundstedt and other German militarists, that during the last war, the striking power of the United States, particularly of their air force, was devastating, continuous and employed with masterful technique.

The earthly component of national greatness has, therefore, been amply demonstrated. What now remains to be achieved is evidence to the world of greatness of mind, refinement of spirit and stability of conduct. The Constitutional Convention of 1787 launched a daring innovation in the science of governing and the art of living, but a new challenge to a different type of leadership confronts us today. The menace of inertia too often lurks concealed behind achieved objectives. We cannot forever be living off the capital of the founding fathers or on the universally respected memory of Washington and Lincoln, or on the literary gifts of Emerson, Thoreau, Orestes Brownson, James Russell Lowell, Henry Adams and William James. Good repute is not an automatic heritage, a supervised trust administered painlessly for heirs at law. It is an open note which must be renewed at the bank by each generation, otherwise it may be unexpectedly called by the holder or secretly bought by an unfriendly competitor. Democracy in particular cannot safely be presupposed; it must be rewon by each generation. Life is growth and time is relentless in discounting the complacency of those who rely on acquired status, place or privilege, or on titles of social and financial position to assure the perpetuity of their tenure. The cycles in nature, the rise and fall of empires and the history of political mutations, from Aristotle to the present day, bear melancholy testimony to the contrary....

The formidable task of controlling the criminal within America is paralleled by the challenge now crystal-clear on the international level. One attempt at World Revolution and the imposition of a Germanic dictatorship was defeated at the cost of millions upon millions of human lives, the dislocation of the world economy, and a continent in ruins. That victory achieved, another claimant to world hegemony now stands, in full armor, knocking at the door of the West.

What we are witnessing and experiencing is one of those transitional periods, one of those great historic crises in the evolution of humanity. It began in 1914 when the accumulation of political, social and economic tensions broke through the thin protective covering of conventional diplomacy and we had World War I. That phase terminated in an armistice, not in order re-established or in equilibrium restored, despite the deceptive solace of peace formalized in treaties and protocols. The tumult in men's souls remained undiminished and was enhanced through the poison of class hatred deliberately introduced into the veins and thinking of bewildered populations since 1919 by the instigators of World Revolution in Moscow. The Twenties and Thirties were wasted in ineffectual attempts to recapture order and achieve a stabilized world economy. The confusion and the fever of discontent, affecting every nation and every government, afforded precious opportunity for the skilled Marxian revolutionist who is taught to work in troubled quarters, particularly on dark nights.

World War II was only the interlude and not yet, I fear, the full climax, in this profound social readjustment, this titanic clash between those elemental forces of life which have been striving from time immemorial to effect a balance between liberty and authority. In the United States we have achieved at least a working synthesis based on acceptance of a Constitution guaranteeing the fundamental liberties of the individual while delegating to government a measure of power, limited and enumerated powers, and endowing it with the authority deemed indispensable to preserve order in the growing complexities of a highly industrialized civilization.

But the transition in Europe was attended with violent convulsions, as the philosophy of total power for government clashed with the inherent postulates of Christianity demanding respect for the dignity of the human personality. The Communist religion, for it is a religion with its own God which is the State, succeeded in imposing its totalitarian creed on the demoralized and exhausted remnants of the Czarist Empire, but encountered stubborn resistance in Central and Western Europe where, for over fifteen centuries, a common culture had resulted in that entity which we call Christendom. The conflict was basic and spiritual as well as social, economic and political. Those who believe it to be a conventional argument over the external forms of social control or economic competition are amateur statesmen and are blind guides to the realities of history.

It is part of the sagacity of the general staff of this world conspiracy to make foreign negotiators believe that it is all a game of conventional power politics, territorial readjustment, economic bargaining and trade agreements. This is understandable, even commendable, from the viewpoint of Machiavelli; but what is incredible is the cowardice of appeasers in attempting to buy a temporary and fallacious security through progressive surrender of decency. So stood the clock of World Revolution on September 1, 1939, when the fallacy of appeasement faced the Frankenstein monster which the faltering diplomacy at Munich had itself created.

World War II, I suggest, was the interlude, the ghastly and inhuman entr'acte, during which Hitler snatched the scepter of World Revolution from the Kremlin and robed himself in the filched trappings of a totalitarian satrap. He strutted his little hour and passed; he was, as it were, a parenthesis in the text of History. His empire crumbled and the scepter has now returned to Moscow; the caravan moves on. That is the external, that is the important aspect of the drama being played out at present on a worldwide stage. Keep your eye on that! The debates and acrimonious controversies at Dumbarton Oaks, in Washington, D.C., San Francisco, Paris and New York were the rear actions, the skirmishes and diversionary maneuvers committed by Mr. Gromyko, Mr. Molotov and Mr. Vishinski in order to cover the main operations in Europe and Asia. The discussions were resumed in March, 1947, at the Moscow Conference and are being continued at present in the council chambers of the United Nations.

It is too early to write a definitive chronology of the Russian Revolution. The primitive dynamism of its energy has been tempered and disciplined by the errors of its adolescent years and every effort is being made to profit from the inertia of the democracies and from the advance in the technicalities of form. The Revolution has made many errors. It initiated numerous experiments and framed three domestic Constitutions. However, certain broad phases may now be recognized: The first period terminated with the seizure of power from the Provisional Government of Alexander Kerensky in 1917 and, obviously, bears the notation "successful." The second phase was of mixed quality: the civil wars, the famine of 1922-1923, the economic debacle that resulted in retreat during the New Economic Policy; the death of Lenin and the Stalin-Trotsky duel made this decade a precarious period internally, while the offensive tactics of the Third International alienated good will abroad and produced one crisis after another. This chapter, broadly considered, must carry the label "unsuccessful." But the Revolution managed to survive. The era of the various Five-Year Plans from 1928 on represents the atmosphere of domestic exaltation and of renewed foreign acceptability. The cooperation with Nazi Germany from 1939 to 1941 advanced the Revolution, both in territory and momentum, until new heights of success were achieved, internal confidence restored and the sights raised. The retreat before the Nazi invasion of 1941 when the two pirates fell out, reduced the Revolution to its lowest point of life expectancy, but the recoil and the achievements of the Red Army in holding Stalingrad and in being allowed to take Berlin rank as "highly successful."

The chapter now in the making is "super-successful" and, though it may not carry the heading "Soviet Geopolitics", it promises to turn out to be the most important geopolitical demonstration of modern times. Something like 270,000 square miles have been added to the Communist Empire; by direct occupation or by indirect control, Soviet power is exercised in Poland, Latvia, Estonia, Lithuania, Romania, Bulgaria, Hungary, Finland, Yugoslavia, Albania, important regions of Austria, Czechoslovakia, Germany, North Korea, Mongolia and Manchuria. By infiltration and fifth column tactics in China, Greece, Italy, France, Palestine, Iran, South America and Afghanistan, attempts are being made to prepare the ground for Communist domination. With respect to population, some 22 million people have been newly brought under Communist control by direct incorporation into the Soviet Union, while a possible 100 million are under her "influence," which differs only in word and pretense from actual domination.

The lines, then, are drawn between absolutism and freedom, between two antagonistic philosophies of life which can no longer be disguised under political pretexts or disputed as technicalities of form or procedure. As evangel of world communism, Soviet Russia is strictly logical in her tactics; she will obscure the underlying issue whenever possible; she will evade, procrastinate and fulminate in the hall of the United Nations; she will refuse to participate in a concert of governments for the economic reconstruction of Europe; she will keep the iron curtain tightly drawn; she will hurl vituperation at everybody who dissents from her self-discovered infallibility. A few days ago she even condoned an open insult against the President of the United States in the pages of her controlled press.

Meanwhile, behind that iron curtain, her war industries are roaring full blast; her armies remain the most powerful aggregation of manpower in the world; her submarines are now formidable in number and quality and her daily increasing supply of airplanes far exceeds the pitiful remnants of vanished American airpower. In her concentration camps an estimated 14 million human beings are held in slave labor, engaged to a very large degree in such significant tasks as the mining of metals, the construction of railroads, canals and airfields, the production of petroleum, cement and pig-iron, the extension of underground structures, fortifications, and similar enlargements of her industrial potential, particularly in the field of heavy industry. Furthermore, the number of her satellites has increased and her agents in the West are now maneuvering for the seizure of power in Italy and France. I am well aware that even a bare recital of these facts is an invitation to be called a warmonger; but that is a hazard to be faced by every man who declines to commit heresy on the altar of dialectical materialism.

Now, does this all mean that what is being prepared will inevitably occur? That there is not the slightest desire to dictatorial power, greed for imperialism or any bellicose intention in the United States is a matter of public record. We have been the givers, not the takers of peace, food, or other peoples' freedom. The contrary charge comes from either ignorance or malice in those who advance the accusation here and from good Leninism in Moscow. But it is not probable that Soviet Russia would deliberately launch an aggressive war against the United States whose power and vast resources are well known to her. Nevertheless, she will continue her war of nerves until, in my opinion, she will have achieved five objectives:

1. Sufficient breathing space to repair the damages inflicted by the Nazi invaders and to permit some modicum of respite to a sorely tried population. Her policy will be to gain time, more time and still more time.

2. The weakening of the prestige of the United States among smaller countries which may be vacillating between East and West. In pursuance of this objective she has launched the current campaign of slander and vituperation.

3. The consolidation of Communism in France and Italy as prelude to a Communist government in both countries.

4. The further infiltration of Communist agents into Latin America and, if possible, into the defense installations of the American Government for the purpose of sabotage in a crisis.

5. Development of uranium in order to produce atomic bombs to match the present strategic advantage of the American Democracy. There can be little doubt that the Soviet Union now has the formula for nuclear fission and blueprints for the bomb; what remains to be done

is the production of the weapons in sufficient quantities to prove effective. That should be possible in less than five years.

In addition, she is anticipating the effect of the coming winter on the shattered European economy with the hope that hunger, cold and general misery will give new force to the ancient Russian proverb: "An empty stomach has no ears." Also, she nourishes the hope and expectation that a depression coupled with inflation of the currency will so cripple the power of America that there will be but one resolute contender left in this historic conflict for survival.

It is not an encouraging message I leave with you on this occasion. I believe it, however, to be an accurate summation of the responsibilities which devolve on you as guardians of the American scene. Your task, as I indicated at the outset, is intimately connected with the successful solution of these international problems. We cannot be secure in an insecure world any more than one individual, however vigorous, can be immune from infection in a plague-stricken city. Conversely, we cannot fulfill our destined role in world affairs unless we are secure at home and strong at home. We cannot prosper in a starving world.

Above all, let us never forget that a weak nation can only beg, not command respect and reciprocity. The periodicity of history has laid on us a challenge to leadership which was not of our seeking but which in cold reality is there. If we decline, someone else stands ready to enter into the breach with a dynamism that will not stop until the dream of Lenin has been realized everywhere. Hence, the parent of civilization of Europe, from which so much of our heritage and culture is derived, now stands expectant and dependent on the vigor of its offspring in the Atlantic World. Now, as never before, we are part and parcel of world destiny, both by commitments to the United Nations and by the shrinking of distance in a shrunken world. Never before, and one need not exclude the critical days of 1939, was there greater need for clear heads, steady hands and great hearts at the controls of human destiny, for men who walk humbly in the sight of God, but keep their powder dry.

A twilight of desperation is settling over Europe from the Thames to the Volga. Continuation of it will not reconcile distressed peoples to the claims of Democracy. After six years of exhausting warfare whole nations are still fearing for their liberties or mourning for them. Where has the Atlantic Charter gone? It thrilled the world in one of its darkest hours with exalted conceptions of freedom, social betterment, equal justice and charity to all peoples of good will. Must we, now in the day of victory, be forced to confess that it was a shoddy campaign device, springes to catch woodcocks? How shall the fate of Poland be reconciled with those two fine passages from President Truman's opening address, on April 25, 1945, to the delegates who drafted the charter of the United Nations at San Francisco: "...If we should merely pay lip service to inspiring ideals and later do violence to simple justice, we would draw down upon us the bitter wrath of generations yet unborn...Justice remains the greatest power on earth. To that tremendous power alone will we submit."

Part II:

International Relations

Father E.A. Walsh, S.J. visiting the Vatican in 1945.

4. See Life Steadily and See It Whole

In May 1934, the University of Delaware celebrated the hundredth anniversary of its founding. In this connection the university sponsored a conference on the issue of the role of the American college in international relations. The choice of the topic reflected the high priority given to international relations by the university, which ranked among the first institutions of higher learning that offered a study abroad program to its students. Representatives of several colleges that offered courses in international relations, including Harvard, Princeton, Sweet Briar, Brown, and Georgetown, were invited to present their views on the function of education in international relations.

At the convocation exercises on May 12, 1934, following the conference, the University of Delaware conferred the honorary degree of Doctor of Laws on Father Walsh.

The kaleidoscopic developments which unfolded in the wake of the First World War also brought about fundamental changes in the conduct of international relations; nationalities in prewar empires emerged as sovereign states, and the development of faster means of communications stimulated commercial transactions and promoted cultural and scientific exchanges. In this new world of a larger community of nations the interests of other countries played a greater role in the formulation of national policies, and planners needed to apply their technical expertise in a broader perspective, with more sensitivity to human needs and to cultural idiosyncracies. "In human relations it is the heart of humanity that must first be won; the head will follow...peace can be maintained, international courtesy assured and the hard-won fruits of civilization preserved only if international relations be based on something more permanent and acceptable than the pragmatic sanction, the increase or decrease of armaments, the predominance of force or the fallacious argument of the 'fait accompli'...." said Father Walsh in his address on "International Peace through International Justice" in May 1932. In this changed economic and political situation, different responsibilities devolved on educators in their task of preparing the younger generation for the challenge.

Father Walsh recognized the new demands and chose as his theme the idea that "one must see life steadily and see it whole," as Matthew Arnold phrased it when characterizing Greek philosophy.

More than fifty years later, in our world of high technology, Father Walsh's emphasis on a liberal education that assures a humanizing element in "the application of factual knowledge to human relations" has proven even more important.

It would doubtless be a twice-told tale in such an assembly as this to enumerate the changes in substance and methods of teaching that have been introduced into education and university perspectives by the historic events of the last twenty years. It is no exaggeration to say that the heavy responsibilities devolving so suddenly on the United States, as an aftermath of that collective insanity called the World War, created national and governmental obligations for which our people as a whole were intellectually and psychologically unprepared. Dislodged from isolated ease and uprooted from our parochial complacency, we were bidden to think and act internationally.

What frequently happens in unforeseen emergencies actually happened to our post-war mentality. Improvisation followed fast and followed faster on the heels of enlarged responsibility. Increasing commitments inevitably followed increased participation in world affairs. Alluring vistas of international service opened up to challenge a nation that previously had been concerned with the tremendous task of solving specific domestic problems caused partly by the Civil War and partly by the ever-increasing industrialization of American society. To be sure, international law and foreign relations had long occupied the attention of scholars and experts, but had left the broad masses of the people untouched and unaffected.

The Spanish-American War, with its concomitant widening of territorial jurisdiction, was only a prelude and a warning forecast of the subsequent phase that swept us, for a decade

---

Speech given at the University of Delaware, Newark, Delaware, on May 11, 1934.

after the Armistice, into a complexity of international relations that needs no rehearsal here. Educators were not slow to recognize their obligations to the new destiny confronting America; interest in foreign affairs and training for a worthy participation in the Golden Age that was to ensue received powerful and widespread stimulus in academic circles. To assist in mobilizing the constructive thoughts and information that should serve as the mainspring for giving direction to national policy was the motive underlying the creation of the School of Foreign Service of Georgetown University, in February of 1919. International peace through international understanding then was and still is the rule of its conduct, as it is also found in the excellent provisions for study in foreign lands included in the curriculum of the University of Delaware.

There are two notions in that expression of purpose, namely, peace and order, which need definition, lest the declared objective be obscured by fascinating but irrelevant and dangerous accidentals. These take the form of special interests, unattainable ideals, laborious technical instrumentalities and emotional exaggerations. The art of the possible in the conduct of international relations is the most realistic definition of diplomacy I have discovered, for it accepts that stern discipline which the facts of history impose on thoughtful men. It reminds the enthusiast and confirms for the cautious that international relations are human phenomena conducted by men among men, not by archangels among disembodied spirits devoid of human passions, free of prejudices, unfettered by racial or national traditions, and superior to the other intangibles that so profoundly modify theory and practice.

Peace, then, like all problems whether practical or speculative, should first be defined. *Ignoti nulla cupido*, runs the wise Latin proverb, there is no desire for the unknown thing. Hence peace begins in the intellect, not primarily in the will which is the principle of external operation. The best definition of peace I know is "the tranquility of order." For where disorder exists, whether in the mental processes or in the moral life of individuals and communities, there is no tranquility of mind. Conversely, where order rules the intellect and will, satisfaction which is only another term for tranquility ensues. International peace, therefore, will result from a satisfactory ordering of rights, obligations, and mutual conduct. We hear much of the rights attaching to nationhood; but we hear less of the obligations resulting from membership in the great family of nations. Yet these are correlative terms and the sovereign rights of one people are the obligations of all others in respect to the possessor. That is the lesson Soviet Russia must learn as she is advancing to full concert with civilized nations.

Order is defined as *apta dispositio plurium ad unum*, the right arrangement of many objects in order to achieve unity of purpose. The chairs in a room are for the use of its occupants and hence are placed in convenient locations on the floor where people may sit on them; they are not suspended from the ceiling, out of reach. And the post-prandial tranquility of a giant beast of prey derives from his having swallowed some weaker animal; that is his idea of the right order of things. Hitherto that has also been Moscow's vision, expressed in appropriate communist language.

If, then, international order implies some controlling goal or objective, it is clear that the effect to be achieved must be independent of and superior to the subjective whims, political ambitions and prejudices of the widely divergent units that make up this world family of approximately two billion restless human beings, assuming, of course, that they wish to live in the social intercourse characteristic of society as organized today. The gunfire of an irresponsible youth at Sarajevo, in the summer of 1914, proved how independent nations are and how sensitive the nerves of the social organisms have become.

The next deduction is inescapable. Should peace be committed to the uncontrolled and arbitrary interpretation of half a hundred individual governments, the antagonisms and clashing of national ambitions and racial prejudices would conspire to produce not order, but chaos. Economic "laissez-faire" and the extreme individualism of the Manchester School have reduced our generation to the present industrial disorder. Similarly, political "laissez-faire" on an international scale resulting in an unreasonable chauvinism brought Western civilization to the brink of the precipice in 1914. I do not see how we can long escape a similar dilemma followed by a more appalling tragedy, unless the nations agree on a principle of fundamental spiritual and moral control. This must be universally applicable, purged of the vicious cynicism of Machiavelli's *Prince* and capable of profoundly moving the depths of man's cultural nature when legalities leave him cold and skeptical. The only standard that can meet these requirements is an awakened sense of international justice, of international respect and mutual toleration. The alternative is the rule of force and a return to the ethics of the jungle. Should an unrelieved and stubborn nationalism become the controlling norm of conduct, I see for the future only a reversion to the narrow localism prevalent in the age of feudalism. Governments and peoples would withdraw behind guarded ramparts, there to devote their energies to the primitive appetites of self preservation, self protection, self sufficiency and selfish national aggrandizement. A glacial cap would settle over civilization and the ice age of international relations would return. So long as the League of Nations, as constituted at the present time, perpetuates the domination of the so-called major powers in the Council over the lesser in the Assembly, it would, in my opinion, be helpless before the steady drift of elemental human forces.

Justice must always extend her jurisdiction from the municipal to the international circuit. Justice in the last analysis simply means rendering to each what is clearly his, *unicuique suum*. There is no infallible public tribunal to resolve that vexed question and to preserve moral equilibrium among men, as we have again learned during the past few years, this time from the Far East. The instinct for justice must be cultivated from below; the seeds must be planted in the hearts, the minds, and the wills of men; it cannot be expected to bloom automatically at the top of the social structure, if it has not roots in the understanding of the people. It is the unending function, then, of education and the spiritual forces of the world to defend this moral substitute for war. It is the responsibility of the independent thinkers of humanity to interpret the appeal of reason and to refuse to be intellectually debauched by fear of the consequences, by political or party considerations, or by the curling lip of professional propagandists.

In a sense, there is no such thing among states as absolute sovereignty. But there is such a thing as sovereign equality, whether possessed by Russia or Geneva, as John Marshall phrased it. So long as man is destined by nature to live in the society of his fellow men, all his rights have a social as well as an individual aspect and no right can be so exercised as to positively injure the common good of the whole community. The sovereign rights of the smallest republic are the reciprocal obligations of the most formidable empire.

Let us be realists without ceasing to be idealists and learn something from the lessons of the past two decades. If hopes for international peace are now at the lowest ebb conceivable, may the disillusionment not be due to the exalted plane to which aspiration was artificially elevated? I am no cynic nor skeptic when I say that one of the most effective enemies to international peace is the opinionated, exaggerated zealot who promises the millenium at the close of his little day. The long record of human nature spread before me forbids me to entertain the hope, however inspirational, that man will leap across centuries, rather than progress by slow toilsome labor, to higher levels of civilized living. Much has been successfully done, particularly in the way of arousing a popular consciousness of the problem, but much remains for the undisclosed future. I for one am far from being discouraged. I know that Christianity, after nineteen centuries, fortified with a divine mandate as it was, and interpreted by the finest minds and voices, has succeeded in persuading only one-third of the human race to accept the new dispensation! It would be the ecstasy of hysteria and the very definition of conceit for us to expect better results within the brief space of one generation.

There is a clear responsibility, therefore, resting both on the students of international relations and the university which undertakes to prepare them for that chosen field. Among those obligations I should count frankness among the first, and honesty, and the ability to see life steadily and see it whole. Technical and specialized information is of the highest importance, but becomes wholly inadequate unless humanized by a broad and liberal background which alone can insure the intelligent and fruitful application of factual knowledge to human relations.... I have long been of the opinion that peace propaganda, in common with democracy and capitalism, must undergo serious revision of its methods. While thoroughly persuaded of the continuing necessity of international peace through international understanding, I am more than ever convinced that the soundest basis on which to build international peace is a tolerant and enlightened nationalism which accepts the historic reality, that few governments have ever been known to confer an unadulterated and purely disinterested favor on another. The opposite contention is a delusion which only time will cure. An emotional and uninformed internationalism may well become dangerous through lack of proportion as the most bumptious and belligerent nationalism.

If ever cool heads and steady hands were needed at the helm of the ships of states and in the public forum which universities provide, it is at the present hour; otherwise the peace of the world lies at the mercy of an accident. Another war, particularly in the prevailing environment of disturbed social conditions and widespread popular discontent, would be suicide as well as homicide for the government deliberately provoking it. And the infection would spread. The only victors would probably be the parties of the extreme left, first in the belligerent, and then in neutral countries, accustomed and trained as they are to fish in muddy waters. The way winds from popular resistance to inspired agitation and then to open revolt. That would mean either an extension of communism or the gradual increase of dictatorships in one form or another; the return of more Caesars cannot but weaken the claims of democracy. I do not suggest that we have or ever did have a mandate to make the world safe for democracy. Woodrow Wilson inverted the order of nature; he should have first have made democracy safe for the world. The universities and colleges of the land, as never before, are on notice that they will be expected to meet the test by furnishing responsible information, temperate judgments and impartial scholarship. The time has come to devote more attention to the production of leaders than to leadership in production.

5. The Future of Pan-American Relations

Over the years a spirit of distrust and suspicion had led to deterioration in the relations between the people of North America and their southern neighbors in the Western Hemisphere. In order to alleviate this tension, President Roosevelt changed the United States policy of direct intervention practised during and after World War I by proclaiming, in his inaugural address in March 1933, a "good neighbor policy," recognizing the Latin American countries' need for equality and dignity. As an indication of the priority he gave to the promotion of goodwill and the increase of understanding among the states of the Western Hemisphere, he directed the U.S. Secretary of State to attend the conference of American States in Montevideo, in December 1933, the first time the chief U.S. Foreign Service officer participated in this series of meetings. As confirmation of their commitment to the new policy, the United States signed, at that meeting, a convention proscribing the interference of any state in the external or internal affairs of another. Furthermore, in an address before the Woodrow Wilson Foundation the same month, the President declared that the United States definitely opposed a policy of armed intervention. Subsequently, American troops were withdrawn from Haiti and the United States no longer interfered in Cuba and Panama. For the first time, financial aid played a part in Pan-Americanism, although some countries resented the new "dollar imperialism."

At the 1936 Buenos Aires Conference, twenty-one American states formed a pact, declaring inadmissible the intervention of any one state, directly or indirectly, and for whatever reason, in the internal and external affairs of any other of the parties. The consensus reached at the 1938 conference in Lima called for consultations among the American states when the peaceful existence of any American republic was threatened. That same year, when the government of Mexico expropriated foreign oil companies, including American-owned firms, the United States met the acid test of the "Good Neighbor Policy" by recognizing the problem as one to be solved solely by Mexico and the businesses concerned.

After the Japanese attack on Pearl Harbor, at the Conference in Rio de Janeiro in January 1942, nearly all the Latin American nations decided to enter the war on the side of the Allies against the Axis countries.

On the eve of the Allied invasion of Normandy, Father Walsh emphasized the importance of unity among the nations of the American continents and the Atlantic area. In later years, when witnessing the cold war in Europe and the hot war in Korea, he restated his belief in the necessity of cordial relations among the peoples of the Americas, in his book *Total Empire*: "The solidarity of the Western Hemisphere is one of the basic conditions for the defense of the Atlantic world. And the continuing freedom of the Atlantic world is the bedrock of confidence for the freedom of the entire world. Weakness or disunion of the Western Hemisphere will mean weakening the course of liberty everywhere."

It is my privilege to greet you on behalf of the two forces which must underlie all true friendship between nations as well as individuals: spiritual kinship and the enlightened understanding which education should achieve. All our deliberations on political, economic and commercial reciprocity will remain sterile and unprofitable unless they are vitalized and sustained by a permanent realization of common ideals and the courtesy of mutual respect.

The necessity for such alliance of mind and heart over and above trade agreements or financial assistance becomes increasingly evident when one contemplates the appalling disaster into which the world has been plunged by the criminal ambitions of the Axis powers. The material hurt to Western civilization and the damage done to the soul of Christendom are apparent and need no rehearsal here. Suffice it to say that at the present time we are facing one of the most profound crises in the history of the human race, a transitional period between two historic epochs when we behold mankind "wandering between two worlds, one dead, the other powerless to be born"....

The menace that is perishing was an evil thing born of arrogance and unholy ambition. If the aggression of the totalitarian powers had succeeded, and how nearly it did succeed, Christianity and democracy might well have been exiled from the continent of Europe to make their final stand here in the New World. By the inscrutable decrees of divine wisdom the assault was thwarted and repulsed at the eleventh

---

Address delivered before the Permanent Council of the Associations of Commerce and Industry–Latin American Section, at the Waldorf Astoria Hotel, New York City, on May 4, 1944.

hour and by a narrow margin. But Europe, the cradle of our civilization and our culture, still lies for the most part under the heel of a ruthless conqueror and bleeds from every vein.

In consequence, a new and heavy responsibility devolves on the shoulders of the New World. The finger of destiny clearly points to the two Americas in the great task of rebirth soon to be inaugurated. Both Christianity and democracy found safe haven there; they have flourished and matured until now when the twenty-one republics of the Western Hemisphere, in the full stature of their manhood, must be prepared to fulfill their trusteeship of both. Liberty is indivisible; wounded in one hemisphere, it is threatened everywhere. Christianity is universal and when menaced in Europe, it is endangered in America. Both Christianity and democracy constitute a heritage that must be newly vindicated by each succeeding generation. That heritage is not an automatic right nor a family heirloom secured forever by the blood and toil and heroism of your ancestors and mine. Like all things of beauty it is a fragile gift and can be smashed to fragments unless consigned to loving hands and guarded in perpetual vigilance by strong hands. It must be bought and paid for by each new beneficiary, but the price is never fully rendered, for it is priceless.

We in the Western Hemisphere have been spared the material destruction and the agony from the air which have devastated the old world. No hostile invader has put foot on these two continents, except for the brief and futile attempt of Japan to secure a foothold in the Aleutian Islands, an adventure that was quickly frustrated and repulsed. No fleets of enemy aircraft have rained down fire and destruction on our cities, our homes, our industrial centers, our libraries, cathedrals, art museums, schools and hospitals.

That favored position leaves America, both North and South, still unimpaired in material structure, economic resources and agricultural productivity. The challenge is to our vision, our courage and our unity. The continental solidarity which Simon Bolivar yearned for, which Henry

Clay attempted and James Blaine initiated, now stands, tiptoe as it were, on the horizon of a new era. Never before did time and circumstance contrive a more inviting opportunity for service to humanity as well as to Pan-American unity. The obstacles which in the past prevented employment of our joint resources and geographical proximity, are now relegated to the limits of old, unhappy memories and misunderstanding on both sides. I shall take the liberty of speaking of these impediments with the complete frankness which should prevail among adult peoples destined by nature and by interest to be true friends.

The suspicion and distrust which characterized so much of Latin American reaction to the United States during the latter part of the 19th century and the early decades of the 20th, derived partly from the attitude of assumed superiority cultivated by certain influential North American writers and by many visitors to the Spanish- and Portuguese-speaking countries of the Southern continent. This psychology ranged from an amused tolerance to a self-righteous indignation and severe criticism of a civilization regarded as backward and reprehensible. There is a subtle residue of historical antagonism in the social and cultural background of North Americans, possibly undetected by the less discriminating critics, which exercises a definite psychological influence over their judgments. The roots of the prevailing North American culture were definitely embedded in Anglo-Saxon traditions. Nothing, descended from Spain and Portugal, could hope for sympathetic treatment from inheritors of traditions dating back to the Spanish Armada, the English Reformation and New England Puritanism. Much of our history was written in that mood and many textbooks used in American educational institutions were vitiated by a biased approach and frequent violence was done to truth and justice. Happily, that prejudice passed away with the passing of the Puritan.

The American Council on Education is at present taking steps to eliminate from textbooks the "black legend" of Spanish colonial cruelty, greed and bigotry which even Bancroft wove into his historical works and which succeeding compilers, petty magazine scribblers and prejudiced lecturers perpetuated in this country. They observed with jaundiced eyes and wrote with hostile minds. They created the fiction that little of culture, progress, art or education was to be found south of the Rio Grande, despite the fact that higher education flourished in many a distinguished school of South America long before John Harvard's academy was founded at Cambridge. San Marco in Peru dates from 1551, for example.... They pictured Latin Americans as plunged in sloth and superstition, and ignored the magnificent contributions made to Christianity by the civilizing influence of the Church, which protected and raised the status of the native Indian population; a sharp contrast to the fanatical zeal of the Puritans, who, on reaching Plymouth Rock, "fell first on their knees and then on the aborigines." Also, they bemoaned the lack of social progress in Spanish America, forgetful or ignorant of the plain historical record which reveals the existence of the Jesuit Republics in Paraguay, those amazing social experiments which for 150 years changed wilderness into democratic utopias, until they were destroyed by the greed of the secular authorities. Of course, such manifestations of concrete Christianity under Latin American auspices were either ignored by or unpalatable to zealots reared in the frigid transcendentalism of Emerson or the naturalism of Thoreau. Fortunately, two Protestant historians of note, Bourne of Harvard and Bolton of the University of California, have contributed substantially to the correction of the ancient prejudices attached to previous writings on Spanish America. By the fairness and quality of their research they rank as pioneers in the field of authentic history.

Several other elements contributed to the deterioration of United States-Latin American relations during the 19th and 20th centuries. The type of American official sent to South and Central America as diplomatic representative in an era and under a system now happily ended, was all too frequently of such inferior caliber as to increase the resentment and hostility of native inhabitants. I think it was O. Henry who began one of his short stories with a revealing flash of local color. A traveller arriving at a Central American port inquires the way to the American consul. He is told: "You will find him either in jail or in the nearest saloon."

Commercial relations with Latin America, with rare exceptions, tended to increase suspicion, fear and distrust. American agents were impatient with local customs and rushed noisily about the land, bent on efficiency and quick profit, careless of sensibilities and often contemptuous of those with whom they dealt. Hence, a quick deal, quick profit and a quick exit became synonymous with the Yankee trader. How often did we hear of these incidents at meetings of the National Foreign Trade Council! And how often did we hear of the unfavorable credit conditions exacted by American exporters in marked difference from the more liberal terms granted by German competitors! Capital investment by Americans was often regarded as a form of government-approved exploitation by an absentee capitalism, whereas English, German, French and some Italian enterprises associated themselves permanently with the fortunes of the country through the welcome spectacle of social adaptation. Their personnel, unlike their transient American competitors, frequently settled in the host country, founded families and became part of the community from which they were deriving their profits.

Then came the fear of imperialism, "dollar diplomacy", and exaggerated interpretations of the Monroe Doctrine which led to more friction in the Caribbean and in Central America. It was not surprising, therefore, that a great Latin American writer, José Enrique Rodó of Uruguay could render an analysis of North America in a style and in a language that made his little book *Ariel* one of the classics of our time. It would well repay frequent re-reading by every American official charged with Latin American affairs. I have derived much fruit from its pages.

While frankly appreciating and enumerating those virtues and achievements of the American character which make them a great people, this thoughtful critic reminds his fellow Latin Americans that greatness is not measured solely by physical stature, mechanical efficiency or towering material civilization. Wealth, power, ceaseless activity and boundless energy provide welcome facilities, to be sure, and guarantee the leisure indispensable for the cultivation of the things of the spirit. But these externalities do not per se constitute good taste, distinction of intelligence or a culture worth imitating or even accepting. That consummation of the North American genius, Rodó claims, remains unfulfilled. The United States, he concludes, still lacks the vital quality of intellectual and spiritual leadership. When the American people of this day and generation will strike the spark which will electrify the world, as those earlier Americans did in 1776 and 1789, then, he prophesies, will their finest potentialities of leadership stand revealed and unchallenged. Then they will not be imposing their utilitarianism and materialism on other peoples who have a specific genius and cherished tradition of their own, but they will be erecting a standard of beauty and spiritual attractiveness to which mankind will voluntarily turn as to a light in darkness.

This conclusion of Rodó suggests certain truths which many thoughtful Americans have long pondered in their heart of hearts: we cannot buy friendship, we can only merit it; we cannot impose leadership, at least not for long, and we must prove our capacity for leadership and demonstrate the superior worth of our program. An enlightened self-interest must persuade all Latin American peoples that their political independence as well as territorial integrity are guaranteed by the pledged power of the United States. But in their social and economic relations, in their internal political organization and in the free development of their specific racial, religious and national culture they must remain the sovereign arbiters of their own destiny. The government of the United States has affirmed categorically that there shall be no more interference in the internal affairs of any Latin American state and ratified the treaties and conventions which established that policy, after the Montevideo Conference. As a symbol of increased respect for the peoples of Latin America, the government of the United States has elevated all its diplomatic posts in those regions to the rank of embassy, a courtesy which has been reciprocated by your governments. During the present global war a special situation exists and abnormal problems arise which must be solved in cooperation with all the members of the Pan-American Union, rather than decided unilaterally by any one party to that Association. In the evolution of military strategy, care must be taken that no permanent advantages be sought which could militate against the good neighbor policy, designed for peace as well as for war.

It must be remembered that several of the larger Latin American communities lie ideologically nearer to the old world than to the United States. As to race, culture and religion, their civilization descends from Spain, Portugal, France, Italy and even from English traditions rather than from Chicago, New York and Washington, D.C. In general, Latin Americans are Catholic, a basic and historic fact which can operate as a stubborn psychological impediment and which has been grossly underestimated. This socio-religious factor in a very delicate equation is further confounded by the unfortunate type of publicity current in Latin America, regarding American manners and morals. Hollywood films of the sensational variety have pictured us in a manner that does little credit to our ideals; divorce statistics reveal a mounting disintegration of marital relations and offend the traditional reverence for family life which has always characterized the Latin American mentality....

Living with one's neighbors, whether they be parochial or continental, is an art, not a science. The textbooks and codes of political science and of investment banking are primarily concerned with forms of government, administrative procedure and rates of return on risked capital. They are not safe guides in the sociology of cultural relations. Human nature will often defy the best calculations of logic, economics and finance and return to the simpler pattern of mutual respect and plain recognition of human personality.

I believe the day of Rodó's vision of the Americas has dawned. The hour has struck for North America to feel the stirrings of that spiritual leadership which, he freely admitted, was the only element lacking to her greatness. She is now mobilized in her wrath and indignation; ten million of her sons stand ready to do battle with the common enemies of mankind wherever found, on land, on the seas, under the waters and in the air. As suffering is the trial by fire that purifies and ennobles individuals, so may this global tragedy ennoble and purify us all, both North and South....

PART III

GEOPOLITICS

At the reunion of former German prisoners of war, Germany, June 1946. From left to right: A german government official; Father E.A. Walsh, S.J.; Col. T.F. Wessels, U.S. Army, one of the administrators of the special project for reorienting German prisoners of war; Dr. Walter Hallstein, president of the University of Frankfurt on Main, later a visiting professor at Georgetown University.

6. Germany's Master Geopolitician

As early as 1924 Father Walsh had become acquainted with the ideas of German geopolitics publicized in the periodical *Zeitschrift für Geopolitik*, which became the mouthpiece for the research organization "Laboratory of World Political Ideas." Its founder and editor, Karl Haushofer, was a military college graduate, who had spent some years in Japan, officially as an instructor to the Japanese army, but actually as observer of the expanding Imperial army. After his return to Germany in 1912 and the publication of two books, on Japan and the Pacific Ocean, he obtained the degree of doctor of geography with the highest distinction. During the First World War he served at the front as a brigadier commander in the German army. Upon Hitler's accession to power Haushofer was appointed president of the German Academy in Munich and became president of the "People's League for Germanism" abroad.

Through his academic teaching and political activity, Haushofer provided the scientific basis for the Nazi revolution and for the struggle for *Lebensraum*. His doctrine was based on his thesis that the leadership of the world rightfully belonged to the Germans and was inspired by Sir Halford Mackinder's theory of the "heartland." Through his friendship with his one-time student, Rudolf Hess, Haushofer came into contact with Hitler and became the political "Nestor of the ruling clique" in Germany.

Some twenty years of attentive study of Haushofer's activities had convinced Father Walsh of the dangerous international objectives underlying his teachings. The world at large realized this only after the outbreak of World War II, when the various invasions broadly followed the plan which Haushofer had consistently expounded. Consequently, after the collapse of the German army, he was considered a security suspect and was to be apprehended to ascertain whether or not he should be tried together with the major war criminals at Nuremberg.

As a renowned scholar of German geopolitics, Father Walsh was a natural choice of the War Crimes Commission to conduct their investigations into the influence of Haushofer's geographic, political and philosophic doctrine on Hitler's national socialism and the aggressive war policy of the Nazis. Following his appointment to that Commission, Father Walsh served as consultant to the United States Chief of Counsel, Supreme Court Justice Robert H. Jackson, at the International Military Tribunal in Nuremberg.

In September 1945, Father Walsh visited Haushofer at his mountain retreat, "Hartschimmelhof," above the Ammer See in Southern Bavaria, to tell him that the Chief Counsel of the United States required his presence at a hearing in Nuremberg. But in view of Haushofer's failing health, exacerbated by a recent heart attack, and only the remote possibility of his being brought to trial, Justice Jackson agreed that Father Walsh should interrogate Haushofer and get him to prepare a final statement on the evil consequences of German geopolitics. Haushofer did submit an *Apologie der deutschen Geopolitik* which was considered the last will and testament of German geopolitics.

In his book *Total Power* Father Walsh analyzes this document and the nature of German geopolitics and also discusses the revolutionary upheavals in Russia, Germany and Japan with which he had become intimately acquainted. Critics welcomed the book as a "most scholarly work," an "authorative study...by a leading geopolitician," an "abundant documentation with primary source material...attractive and enlightening reading," and as a "...powerful book on the struggle for absolute power in the modern world." As additional tribute, a reviewer pointed out that "... The American public is doubly indebted to Father Walsh for this work...," which might have been lost in a fire at Mulledy Hall (the Jesuit residence at Georgetown University) in February 1947, "... had he not run in at great personal risk to save it from the flames." (*Courant*, Hartford, Conn., *Press*, Pittsburgh; *Best Sellers*, Scranton University; *Dispatch*, Columbus, Ohio; *The Evening Star*, Washington, D.C.)

In chapters IV and V Father Walsh recalls Professor Haushofer's last days and examines the basic tenets and political implications of his doctrine.

Chapter IV

The End of Professor General Karl Haushofer

During November and December other duties at Nuremberg, Frankfurt, Fulda, Berlin, Münster, Cologne, Rhineland and Wiesbaden made it impractical to visit Haushofer again in South Bavaria. But several letters arrived from him dealing with the future of Germany under the occupation, with the proposed land reform in the American zone as compared with the Russian pattern in East Prussia, and with certain problems concerning his personal status under the de-Nazification Law. His desire to cooperate and redeem the promise made at Nuremberg seemed sincere and authentic. He furnished many valuable leads, particularly in respect to the missing documents and diaries of his son Albrecht—a collection of records which he warned me should be tracked down, since Albrecht had maintained the closest relations with the Nazi Foreign Office and had lost his life because of his efforts to negotiate peace as early as 1941 through intermediaries in Switzerland.

A long communication dated November 12 was, in effect, a geopolitical analysis of conditions in Bavaria. "Because I know all this," he wrote, *"dixi et salvavi animam meam,"* meaning "I have spoken out and saved my soul."

"Since I had not hesitated to speak the truth to the illegitimate rulers of the Third Reich—the truth I had struggled for

---

Chapters IV and V from *Total Power–A Footnote to History*, by Edmund A. Walsh, S.J. Published by Doubleday & Company, Inc., Garden City, New York, 1948. Reprinted by permission.

painstakingly and in a hard way—I now believe I must speak the truth to the highest American authority I can reach. Otherwise you might think: Who knows the truth and speaks it not is a villain....Around your oak the snow lies deep; but the tree reminds me continually of one of the deepest influences of my life, for which I thank you."

The reference to the oak tree recalled an incident that exemplified the strange blend of romanticism and hard pragmatism which characterized Haushofer's mind. He had led me one day to a pleasant spot on his property from which one had a commanding view of the lake and the encircling hills. A sturdy oak dominated the landscape; at its base, he said, he often sat and meditated. "This tree from this day onward shall bear your name," he announced.

A letter dated November 23, in English, from Martha Haushofer, his wife, brought the news that Haushofer had suffered a serious stroke. "At first his right arm and leg were paralyzed and he could scarcely speak; today that has improved, and the doctor says there is no imminent danger. But of course the attack can repeat itself at any time and probably he will not be able to do any brainwork or walk normally. All that is very sad, as you can imagine. But to the bodily sickness is added the chronic worry about his position with regard to political matters. He has been left unmolested, as you had promised...but his name has seemingly not yet been removed from the list of war criminals."

Not long after, in a note dated November 25, she wrote, "The trouble is increasing: local officials of the American Counter Intelligence Corps appeared at Hartschimmelhof with a new order for his arrest." She managed to persuade them that he was helpless upstairs and any such announcement "would certainly mean killing him outright." The order was modified to "house arrest," and later negotiations on my part resulted in Haushofer's being allowed to continue in ignorance of the new developments—which had been owing to certain local denunciations, of which the Third Army felt obliged to take cognizance.

Evidently his mental powers slowly returned, as a letter dated December 29 arrived at Nuremberg in early January just as I had returned from a month's absence in North Germany in search of evidence of religious persecution under the Nazi regime.

He wrote:

Dear Professor Walsh:

> The fateful year of 1945 is drawing to an end. It has brought upon my country and my people the worst catastrophe for centuries, and to myself more grief than any other in my long life. Looking back on so much darkness, the few gleams of light seem all the more consoling and I feel doubly grateful for every mark of kindness and understanding, and all the more so when they come from a chivalrous, scientific opponent. Your name will always be connected in my remembrance with one of the few redeeming features of this year.

He then undertook to recount some of the new annoyances that had been visited on him, but came back again to his oft-repeated reference to the documents of his son Albrecht, which had been hidden in a third house owned by the family in the mountains near Garmisch-Partenkirchen.

He ended with the sentiment:

> One of the greatest joys the New Year could bring me would be a meeting with you, and I hope that you will be able to keep your promise and come to see me once more. You will always find me at home, as I am not able to move from here.

> For yourself, my best and earnest wish is that you may attain some of the ideals toward humanitar-

ian progress for which you are striving and so benefit our suffering fellow creatures all over the world.

[Sgd] Dr. Karl Haushofer

His letter of February 7, 1946, is filled with indignation at the news that Rudolf Hess had stood up in court at Nuremberg and admitted that his amnesia had been a trick, a simulated condition "for tactical reasons." Haushofer let go both barrels at his protégé and favorite pupil:

...and above all, you will understand the news about Hess and his contradictory behavior occupied my mind, yes, even excited me inwardly very much. Since the confrontation at that time, which touched me deeply and moved me much more than I allowed myself to show, this behavior, I say, brought me one puzzle after another. On that occasion I was so thoroughly convinced that his not recognizing an old friend was genuine that I attributed it to a serious emotional disturbance. Then I had to learn that he, himself, admitted that he had simulated it and that he now felt well enough to defend himself personally. Afterward, as before, I regret profoundly that in his own interest he let slip by that one chance of possibly improving his situation during that conversation in your presence. As for myself, I am now completely at a loss regarding Hess, and even if I should be called as a witness, I could not say anything else in his case but a resigned *non liquet* [it is not clear], because through his own inexplicable behavior the ground is cut completely from beneath my feet—the ground for just judgment.

I feel I owe you this explanation, inasmuch as you attended—with so much human gentleness, this conference which was more than embarrassing, indeed terribly painful for me.

In the same letter he returned with insistence to the importance of finding those hidden documents of his son Albrecht. Certain secret papers of Hitler had recently been deciphered at Nuremberg, setting forth the details and circumstances of Albrecht Haushofer's peace overtures as far back as 1941. Portions of these revelations were reported in current German newspapers.

"This clearly shows," wrote Haushofer, "that our son became the victim of his honorable endeavors to put an end to the struggle as early as 1941, and he probably, yes, certainly, lost his life as a result of what he attempted to do at that time."

This letter terminates on a particularly poignant note:

> About myself not very much can be said. I live, or rather I keep on vegetating quietly. At my age the consequences of a stroke cannot be erased any more. I suffer much pain and sleep little....If I still have an earnest wish in the span of life yet left, which I hope will not be for long, it will be the hope of seeing you and talking to you once more, this time with more quiet and at greater length than was possible when you hurried through on your way back from Italy. Should you be able to meet my wish, please do not put it too far off.

Two phrases in this letter gave me pause: "...the span of life yet left, which I hope will not be for long," and his earnest desire to see me again: "...please do not put it too far off."

That decided me. An airplane flight to Czechoslovakia in late January 1946 had given me the opportunity for a conference with President Beneš, who confirmed the activities of Albrecht Haushofer when sent as Hitler's emissary to Prague during the pre-Munich negotiations. The historical importance of Albrecht's diaries was thus becoming more and more evident; but prior commitments connected with my main obligation of obtaining evidence of the Nazi persecution of Christianity required postponement of my next long-delayed conference with Haushofer.

A hurried excursion into northern Hesse on the trail of documents was completed by February 22, and Hartschimmelhof was next on my itinerary. But a new and unforeseen obstacle now intervened—Nature herself. It was still winter, and the roads off the main highways beyond Starnberg were deep in snow. Arriving within five miles of Haushofer's farm above Lake Ammer on Sunday, February 24, our automobile bogged down three times in deep drifts into which we had wandered through inability to see the road hidden under the shifting banks of snow. Twice my G.I. and myself were obliged to enlist the brawn of nearby Bavarian farmers to shovel us out of the trap and then spread gravel under our churning tires, as we had no chains. But the last mischance gave cause for alarm. Nothing availed to move our sedan. We were alone some place between Erling and the slow ascent leading to Hartschimmelhof. We could only sit inside the sedan as protection against the icy wind and debate the problem. After some forty-five minutes we heard the welcome chugging of a tractor nearby and were relieved beyond expression when the Bavarian driver agreed to being requisitioned as a towing agent. Once out of the ditch, my G.I. respectfully but firmly rebelled: "This has happened three times, sir. We can never make that next slope, and if we get bogged down in that forest over yonder in this weather it could be very serious. We might be out here all night, which would be bad for many reasons, especially on the security side. An American patrol may not pass this way for an indefinite time. I cannot take the responsibility."

He was right, and I regretfully instructed him to head back toward Munich. That decision meant that I was never to see Haushofer again. I waited for the weather to abate and the snow to disappear from the less frequented roads, utilizing the interval for renewed work at Salzburg and Vienna in connection with the Nazi persecution of the Church in Austria. But death came sooner than the thaws of spring.

On March 14 the news reached me that Haushofer and his sixty-nine-year-old wife had committed suicide on the previous Sunday. Proceeding immediately to Hartschimmelhof and seated that evening with Haushofer's only surviving son Heinz in the geopolitician's library, with all the paraphernalia of his scholarship strewn around us, I heard an amazing recital, and later retraced each step outdoors in reconstructing the tragedy as it progressed from the house on the hill to journey's end in the gully near the road.

The written statement delivered to me by Heinz Haushofer for the records at Nuremberg declares that the idea of suicide had been constantly present in his father's thoughts for several years, indeed from 1941.

> Even at that date my father clearly foresaw the approaching catastrophe of the Hitler regime; moreover, the flight of his former pupil, Hess, deprived him of his sole protection against the distrust and persecution of the radical wing of the National Socialist movement. Consideration for his sons and grandchildren prevented him from bringing his intended suicide to realization, as without him they would have been without any protection and would have been exposed to even a greater extent also, because of their non-Aryan origin....Already, at that time, that is, after my return [from prison], he would have liked to end his life if the process of his own justification in the eyes of the Forces of Occupation had not begun. In many talks with him, often lasting for hours, we saw clearly again and again that suicide in those circumstances would have been a sign of cowardice and of bad conscience. But my father did not want to evade this point-by-point discussion of his lifework.

> Although he recovered physically after the stroke, it was clearly noticeable—and he personally was also conscious of it—that his mental capacities slackened for a man of his lifelong working powers and intensity; especially did the deterioration of his memory and of his ability to

express himself depress him deeply. Daily in his talks with me the thought of suicide intruded itself again and again, and he explained that he intended to wait for things to clear up finally, things concerning the future of his family....It is self-evident that I, as a son, was always opposed to these utterances of my father and often in discussions which lasted for hours I fought with him on the question whether suicide—from the ethical point of view—is permissible or not. Opposing the Christian point of view, which I represented, he claimed for himself the right of the stoic, to be allowed to end his life after having fulfilled his duties....The initiative for this joint suicide of my parents without doubt originated with my father; since my parents had lived together for fifty years in unparalleled faithfulness, my mother decided to go with him at the same time, in a *matrimonium mortis*, as the Romans expressed it.

Both my parents left letters behind for me in which the facts I have mentioned are verified quite unequivocally. On the evening of their suicide my father, moreover, sent a letter to Professor Walsh in Nuremberg, the contents of which I do not know.

On the morning of March 10, [sic] 1946, I, myself, found my parents, my father poisoned and my mother poisoned and hanged.

[Sgd] Heinz Haushofer
Hartschimmelhof, Bavaria
14 March 1946

Written and signed in my presence,
Hartschimmelhof, Bavaria
14 March 1946
[Sgd] Edmund A. Walsh

The execution of the suicide pact was marked by a meticulous attention to details. On Monday morning, March 11, the son awaited his mother downstairs, as a journey had been arranged to the nearby town of Weilheim. As neither of his parents appeared, he investigated and found their beds had not been slept in; the letters of farewell were on the pillow, together with a neatly drawn diagram showing where the bodies would be found. It appears that the pair, who were shortly to celebrate the fiftieth anniversary of their marriage, had quietly slipped out of the house some time late Sunday night when the household had retired and made their way in darkness down a dirt road for something like eight hundred meters, nearly half a mile, to the chosen spot. It was a secluded hollow on the estate, through which flowed a small stream approximately four feet wide. A tree grew on the bank, one stout limb projecting over the water. This unfrequented ravine presumably had been carefully selected, as Heinz some time previously had found a poem describing that particular tree in his father's sketchbook, together with an illustration of it drawn by his own skilled hand.

They must have reached their rendezvous with death at approximately 11 P.M., as the state of the bodies when found next morning permitted the medical examiner to estimate the number of hours which had elapsed since *rigor mortis* had set in. Martha Haushofer's body was hanging by the neck from the tree. They had both taken arsenic as well (mixed in a cordial), but Haushofer had evidently been prevented by his bodily weakness from making assurance doubly sure after taking the poison. His body lay sprawled on the ground, face down, his feet toward the creek, his hands clutching the Bavarian soil which he so passionately loved and so often described in his writings on *Lebensraum*. In his *Apology of German Geopolitics* he had used the expression, "the sacrament of the earth."

The lantern, with the extinguished candle which had lighted them through the darkness, lay beside them. Traversing their route step by step a few days after the double suicide—it was on the Ides of March—and attempting to reconstruct the scene as it was played out on that windy March night on one of the loneliest hillsides in Bavaria, I could only liken it to some final act of a Greek tragedy. As if to seal his name and his lifework in complete oblivion he left instructions to his son that no marker, memorial, or other form of identification should ever be placed on or near his grave.

Chapter V

Last Will and Testament of German Geopolitics

The document handed to me by Haushofer on November 2, 1945, four months before his suicide, was, in effect, the last will and testament of German geopolitics. The contents were made public for the first time at an address delivered at the University of Frankfurt, Germany, on June 18, 1946, in the form of a report authorized by Justice Jackson. On that occasion the complete text was first read to the *Forum Academicum* by a member of the faculty, Professor Willy Hartner, and was followed by a statement in which I set forth what was acceptable and what was unacceptable in this last exposition of doctrine by the greatest and the last of the Nazi geopoliticians.

The document recounts the rise and fall of German geopolitics in an intensely human and personal recital, during which Haushofer protests that Hitler and his colleagues grossly distorted the scientific and valid part of his geographical theories and popularized them in fanatical language in order to justify aggressions and invasions never intended by Haushofer. Moreover, he writes, all that was written after 1933 was under great pressure and must be judged accordingly. His wife was a half-Jewess and consequently was forever under the menace of being transported to Theresienstadt, a concentration camp, or to Auschwitz, where 2,500,000 human beings were put to death. His former pupil, Rudolf Hess, was the sole protector of his wife's existence, and when Hess fled to England, their last bulwark was gone. "In the Third Reich the party in power lacked any official organ receptive to or understanding [of] the doctrines of geopolitics. Therefore they only selected and wrongly interpreted catchwords which they did not comprehend. Only Rudolf Hess, from the time he was my pupil, before the National Socialist party even existed, and the Minister for Foreign Affairs, Von Neurath, had a certain understanding for geopolitics—without being able to apply it successfully."

Haushofer cites numerous scholars in America and England in support of his basic teaching: Captain Mahan of the United States Navy, Brooks Adams, Ellen Churchill Semple, Isaiah Bowman, president of Johns Hopkins University, and Sir Halford Mackinder, whose theory of the "Heartland" was frequently cited in Haushofer's writings. Hitler's Eastern policy, i.e., his Russian adventure, is described as a "deadly sin" against both geopolitics and correct statesmanship. Haushofer declares that a "seesaw between oceanic and continental powers was grossly misunderstood in the Third Reich." He points out that after 1938 he was in disgrace with Hitler because he had tried to dissuade the Führer from the dangerous policy he was then contemplating. He cites his imprisonment in Dachau in 1944; how his eldest son Albrecht was murdered by the Gestapo in 1945; his second son Heinz was imprisoned, as were also other members of his family. The work of a lifetime was ruined and his health seriously impaired.

The testament includes a denial of the charge that Haushofer assisted Hitler to write *Mein Kampf*. With some indignation he protests that he had nothing to do with that performance and saw the book only after it appeared in print. One has only to compare his style with Hitler's way of writing! He refused to review *Mein Kampf* in his journal, *Zeitschrift für Geopolitik*, because "it had nothing to do with geopolitics." It was Hess, not Hitler, who came directly under his personal influence, Haushofer asserted, and the ideas thus transmitted were distorted and abused by the Nazi leaders. He protests that he never saw Hitler alone or in private. His admiration for Japan and his activities in that field are described as cultural only, with no intention of encouraging military aggression. The fact that he had been invited by foreign statesmen and learned societies to lecture in many of the capitals of Europe must indicate, he argues, that he was not considered an unreasonable person; on the contrary, he was *persona grata* in Vienna, Rome, Prague, Budapest, Reval, Geneva, Oxford, and Lisbon.

Many errors were made, Haushofer admits, but he insists that he never advocated the violent and unilateral military policy of Hitler. He makes an earnest plea for co-operation among the scholars of the world to establish a true and legitimate geopolitics based on international understanding and respect for human rights. He ends his apologia with the aspiration: "Granting that errors and mistakes accompanied the course of geopolitics, they can be turned to profit by the wisdom of that saying in the English language—'All progress resolves itself into the building of new roads.'"

I agreed with Haushofer's chronology of geopolitics in modern Germany and the legitimate function it can exercise in supplying a helpful and informative body of knowledge for the guidance of statesmen in the formulation of domestic policy and the conduct of international relations. Geography undoubtedly is one of the basic physical factors which influence the political institutions of a people; it is likewise [a] matter of historical record that the geographic features of a country—position, size, land forms, climate and natural resources—have deeply influenced the quality and evolution of its foreign policy. History abounds with examples. The limitations imposed on the English people by the confining character of their island space became a very definite factor in the historical growth of the British Empire. The small and limited principality of Moscow, as it originally existed under the Ivans, expanded in response to that urge for outlet to the sea which eventually created the sprawling Russian Empire. Geography admittedly played an important role in the territorial and political imperialism which resulted in the march of the double-headed eagle even beyond Siberia to the west coast of North America in the nineteenth century and to the very front door of the Japanese Empire in the twentieth century. But geography was not then the only motive, as it is not the sole motive in the foreign policy of present-day Russia.

Geography was admitted by Aristotle to be a prime consideration—though not the sole determinant—in the political science of his day and of every generation. In his *Politics*, Books II, III, and VII, he descants on the influence of location, climate, soil, topography, and environmental geography in general as factors of political import in the life of a state. Strabo, the Greek geographer who wrote at the beginning of the Christian era (63 B.C.-A.D. 21), was probably the first conscious geopolitician, as he composed a geographical treatise which he hoped would serve the needs of states and become a useful guide for the statesman as well as for the public at large.

The Middle Ages had their Albertus Magnus, whose geographical knowledge went far beyond his times; he even predicted that a canal would one day be cut at Suez. Montesquieu, in his *De l' Esprit des Lois*, has a vast amount on the role of topography, climate, and other environmental factors in imparting specific character to the legal institutions of a given civilization. Immanuel Kant went so far as to assert that geography is the basis of history. Such a thesis, though susceptible of exaggeration by enthusiasts, finds persuasive application at many points.

Thus the geopolitical position of Holland at the mouth of the most important river system of western Europe made it a focal point of trade and commerce, while its seacoast provided strategically located ports and terminals for the merchant ships of one of the world's most active sea routes. The resultant genius and instinct for seafaring reached as far as Asiatic waters, and a Dutch Empire arose in the Indies which conferred on Holland a power potential wholly disproportionate to the tiny homeland in northwestern Europe.

At the beginning of the nineteenth century Baron Dietrich Heinrich von Bülow was called "the mad baron" because of his geopolitics, and so alarmed the monarchs of Europe that the Russian Czar clapped him into a dungeon at Riga, where he conveniently expired. Anticipating Professor Renner of Columbia University, von Bülow had divided continental Europe into twelve viable states—though Renner would allow only nine in 1942.

Thomas Jefferson's acquisition of Louisiana in 1803 was geopolitics in its very definition. To secure one key city and an open port for the exports of the Mississippi Valley he purchased an empire and suggested to Congress that it overlook "metaphysical subtleties." The celebrated Russian historian, V. O. Klyuchevsky, wrote his monumental *Course of Russian History* from a geopolitical point of view, as he declares in his opening chapter without specifically mentioning the word. Seward's purchase of Alaska in 1867 and his subsequent interest in Greenland gave far more evidence of politico-geographic acumen than is commonly attributed to that tempestuous member of Lincoln's cabinet. Frederic Jackson Turner's "*The Significance of the Frontier in American History*" was a striking geopolitical monograph. Theodore Roosevelt had a very practical understanding of geopolitics as applied to the Isthmus of Panama. And surely Homer Lea—that amazing adventurer from California who became American military adviser to the Chinese Government and who, as early as 1909, prophesied in minute detail the strategic stages in the Japanese attack on the Philippines in 1941—had as keen a sense of "political torsions in the monsoon lands" as Haushofer ever had. All these precursors of the Munich specialist lacked only classification; they were geopoliticians without portfolio.

But beginning with Karl Ritter (1779-1859) we detect the first stages in the corruption of pure geopolitical knowledge in favor of the political objectives of imperialistic governments. The organic conception of the state—which Ritter favored—is the basic geographic heresy that led to the irrational and one-sided policy of German geopoliticians during the Nazi regime. This concept, which was later elaborated by Ratzel in his seven laws on the spatial growth of states—*Uber die Gesetze des Räumlichen Wachstums der Staaten*—was accepted by Karl Haushofer and became the justification for Hitler's claim to *Lebensraum* at any price, even at the cost of the rights of other nations to existence and in violation of their legitimate national sovereignty. Conceiving the state as an organism in nature which must grow and grow and never remain static, this school of political science, at least in its extreme form, was forced by the logic of its position to justify conquest as a biological necessity. Thus Haushofer approved the various stages of any expanding Japanese imperialism as the "rhythmical breathing of a continuously expanding life organ."

While agreeing with Karl Haushofer in a great percentage of his geographical teachings, I took sharp issue with him on many of the political implications of his theories and writings. The same reservations were repeated in the address at the University of Frankfurt. His description of his predecessors among English, French, Swedish, and American geographers is accurate and historically correct. The evidence also points to a distinct change in his personal relations to high Nazis after 1938, and his subsequent treatment by them has been confirmed from independent sources.

Thus we have direct confirmation of Haushofer's statement that he was actually out of favor for a considerable period before 1944. A captured document signed by Martin Bormann, head of the Party Chancellery, and addressed to Rosenberg, in his capacity as supervisor of the Intellectual and Spiritual Formation of the National Socialist party, urges Rosenberg to minimize Haushofer's influence in the estimation of the public. This letter reads:

The Führer's Headquarters
17 June 1942

Highly Esteemed Party Member Rosenberg—

I have been informed that Professor Doctor Karl Haushofer was very prominently featured in the last number of the *National Socialist Monthly* magazine. It was on the occasion of a book review of his work on war geopolitics, in which the reviewer came to the conclusion that this book must by no means be overlooked.

I am of the opinion that Professor Karl Haushofer and also his son, Professor Albrecht Haushofer, should no longer be given any publicity and I would be thankful if you, too, would join in this decision. I would request information as to your position and conclusion in the matter. Heil Hitler!

Yours,
M. Bormann

One can also accept Haushofer's expressed desire to co-operate in a humane and universal organization of good will for the preservation of world peace. His estimate of his professional standing in European learned societies and academic circles is warranted by the facts of his record; also his refusal to associate himself with anti-Semitism as a policy, although—probably for the sake of prudence—he permitted himself to indulge in occasional very harsh abuse of Jews as a group. In this he succumbed to the fashion of the hour. One of his colleagues, writing in the *Zeitschrift für Geopolitik* (of which Haushofer was editor) strove to be vituperative, but only succeeded in being ridiculous. In the September 1938 number, page 776, he refers contemptuously to "the Jewish actor, George M. Cohan."

I also subscribed to the very large degree of validity to be found in Haushofer's factual and doctrinal exposition of the geographical elements of an enlightened national policy. I admitted to him, as I did to my German audience in Frankfurt, that he often reached 50 percent or somewhat better of sound truth. In his "Defense" he raises my estimate to 70 percent, a wholly understandable effort at self-justification. Mathematical computation of the proportion between the good and the evil elements in any policy is merely a way of speaking; the evil element may, in fact, be only 10 percent by bulk, but its weight may sink the vessel. That is exactly what happened to German geopolitics. Fully aware of the weight of other imponderables such as psychology, tradition, special interest, economics, religion, commerce, race, and cultural loyalties, Haushofer himself in an unguarded moment admitted that geography accounts for "about one quarter" of the motivation entering into policy making in a state. But in the face of his own reasoning he obstinately made geopolitics a panacea for all problems of international relations. He established another of those single-answer schools, the over-simplifiers, who were once described so shrewdly by Henry Adams: "Forty years ago our friends always explained things and had the cosmos down to a point."

I disagreed vigorously with Haushofer's contention that his ideas were violently distorted and abused by Hitler against the wishes and intent of their author. If he felt in 1945, while under interrogation, that his teachings had been abused, long before that date he had endorsed the use which later was made of them by the Führer. Thus, in *Welt Politik von Heute*, page 115, ff., he holds that small states have practically no right to exist: Survival of small states, he maintains, is a clear sign of world political stagnation. Absorption, on the other hand, indicates life and development. That is precisely what the Nazi program sought to accomplish. It simply executed in the concrete and with brutal logicality the master pattern advocated by Haushofer.

His specific denial of complicity with Hitler in writing *Mein Kampf* is correct in a technical sense. What he contributed at a given point in Hitler's psychological evolution was a line of argument, a thesis, and a series of geographical facts heavily weighted with political significance. Hitler's earlier speeches were in the demagogic tradition: impassioned denunciation of Versailles, ridicule of the Weimar Republic, references to the menace of Bolshevism, indictment of Jews and world Jewry, attacks on the democracy of Western Powers, exaltation of Germanic blood, appeals to German honor—and a crusade of revenge for the "stab in the back." But in *Mein Kampf* a new strain appears. In addition to the old clichés we find frequent invocation of *Lebensraum*, discussions of the relationship between living area and outward security, evaluation of space as furnishing depth in defense, appeals for natural frontiers, a balancing of land power versus sea power, and the place of geography in military strategy. This graduation from rabble-rousing to the elementary stages of geopolitics is too striking and too circumstantial to be a mere coincidence, in view of the type of reading matter that Haushofer admitted he had brought to Hitler and Hess in Landsberg prison. In Chapter XIV of *Mein Kampf* one can almost feel the presence of Karl Haushofer, although the lines were written by Hess at the dictation of Hitler. What Haushofer did was to hand over a sheathed sword of conquest from his arsenal of scholarly research. Hitler unsheathed the blade, sharpened the edge, and threw away the scabbard.

Similarly, Haushofer's explanation that his commendation of Japan's aggressiveness was meant only as approval of her cultural aspirations is not the whole truth. He went much further than that. His admiration for Japan and his endorsement of her policy as something to be imitated by Germany had military implications, since Japan, he hoped, would become the forefront of "a punishing justice...to be felt by our merciless economic and political enemies and oppressors." Co-operation with Japan in expelling the white man from Asia would be a "symbiosis of cultural politics." He pictured Japan as a revolutionary Nemesis in the Orient as Germany would become in the west. (*Geopolitics of the Pacific Ocean*, 1924, page 162; *Zeitschrift für Geopolitik*, 1938, page 820.) That Haushofer did not proceed to the overt act of enlisting Japan to help Germany's military conquests is possibly true. That was left to Von Ribbentrop. But it is highly significant that it was in Haushofer's house, in Munich, that conferences were held in prewar days between high Nazi officials and important Japanese statesmen and admirals. The fact of these conferences was admitted to me by Haushofer, but the claim was made that they were merely talks on "cultural co-operation."

As no stenographic record of these "cultural" conversations is available, we are not in a position to evaluate their content. But we do have a detailed report of certain subsequent developments when Nazi diplomacy took over after Haushofer had laid the groundwork. Among the 700 tons of captured enemy documents were found the minutes of a conversation between the Reich Minister for Foreign Affairs, Von Ribbentrop, and the visiting Japanese Foreign Minister, Matsuoka, held at Berlin on March 29, 1941. The document is indexed at Nuremberg as U.S. Document 1877–PS. These negotiations between the ministers of foreign affairs of the two major Axis Powers took place, it will be noted, several months before the German invasion of Russia and some eight months before the Japanese surprise attack on Pearl Harbor.

Von Ribbentrop cautions his Japanese ally not to go too far in the impending talks with the Russians in Moscow, as a German-Soviet war was not out of the realm of possibility. But he assures Matsuoka that Germany would attack Russia immediately if Moscow should ever attack Japan. Hence Matsuoka was encouraged to continue to push forward to the south, especially on Singapore. On Matsuoka's expressing Japan's fears concerning an American submarine attack from the Philippines and British naval intervention, Von Ribbentrop replied that the British Navy would have its hands so full in the Mediterranean and home waters that not a ship could be spared for the Far East. Admiral Raeder, whom Ribbentrop had consulted on that aspect, had, moreover, reported that the American submarines were "so bad that Japan need not bother about them at all." Matsuoka agreed that the Japanese Navy had a very low opinion of the British Fleet, but was worried about the Americans. He explained the latter point by saying that Japanese naval experts feared that the Americans would not risk their fleet in operations against Japan and hence "the conflict with the United States might perhaps be dragged out to five years. This possibility caused considerable worry in Japan."

Von Ribbentrop comforted him on that point, showing how America could do nothing in the event of the capture of Singapore, as Roosevelt would think twice about the question of prestige involved in the probable loss of the Philippines. Anyhow, the Americans were not ready and had no adequate armament. Matsuoka, with gusto, then explained that he was doing everything possible to tranquilize the English about Singapore, acting "as if Japan had no intentions at all regarding this key position of England in the East. Therefore it might be possible that his attitude toward the British would appear to be friendly in words and acts. However, Germany should not be deceived by that. He assumed this attitude not only to reassure the British but also in order to fool the pro-British and pro-American elements [in Japan], until one day he would suddenly open the attack on Singapore." This, he felt, would unite the entire Japanese nation by a single act. "Nothing succeeds like success," Von Ribbentrop interjected.

Matsuoka finally came to the milk in his coconut: Would Germany give written assurance of assistance? Von Ribbentrop parried and fenced by replying that this question had already been discussed with the Japanese Ambassador Oshima. He then requested Matsuoka to furnish maps of Singapore "in order that the Führer—who probably must be considered the greatest expert on military questions at the present time—could advise Japan on the best method of attack against Singapore." He also promised to put at Japan's disposal German experts on aerial warfare who now had great experience in the use of dive bombing. As for the fortification at Singapore, Von Ribbentrop again invoked the military genius of Hitler: "...the Führer had developed new methods for the German attacks on strongly fortified positions, such as the Maginot Line and Fort Eben Emael [Belgium], which he could make available to the Japanese."

This conspiracy, which dotted the "i's" and crossed the "t's" of Haushofer's academic spadework, was resumed on April 5, 1941, as set forth in U.S. Document 1882–PS and signed by Schmidt, the well-known Nazi interpreter. Matsuoka remarked on that occasion that the intellectuals of Japan "still exercised considerable influence." Von Ribbentrop characterized intellectuals as a luxury "most of whom are parasites, anyway....The intellectuals ruined France; in Germany they had already started their pernicious activities when National Socialism put a stop to them; they will surely be the cause of the downfall of Britain, which is to be expected with certainty." In concluding his remarks, the Reich Foreign Minister summarized the points he would have Matsuoka take back to Japan from his visit to Berlin:

1. Germany had already won the war. With the end of this year the world would realize this. Even England would have to concede it, if it had not collapsed before then, and America would also have to resign herself to this fact.

2. There were no conflicting interests between Japan and Germany. The future of both countries could be regulated for the long run on the basis that Japan should predominate in the Far East and Germany in Europe and Africa.

3. Whatever might happen, Germany would win the war. But it would hasten victory if Japan would enter the conflict. Such an entry into the war was undoubtedly more in the interest of Japan than in that of Germany, for it offered a unique opportunity, which would hardly

ever return, for the fulfillment of the national objectives of Japan—a chance which would make it possible for her to play a really leading role in East Asia.

Matsuoka replied that he himself could only repeat that he had long been of the opinion that every nation would be offered an opportunity only once in a thousand years. Japan was confronting such an opportunity, and she would have to assume the risk connected with it. She would have to act decisively at the right moment in order to take advantage of this unique opportunity.*

But to return to Haushofer. We find more than merely cultural sympathy in the blanket endorsement of Hitler's policies which he gives in *Welt Politik von Heute*, page 22 and ff.: "Every one of us is somehow an actor on the stage of world politics. Even in the most humble place, as the willing follower of a God-given leader, we help shape the future of our people, be it only by the right echo at the right time and place. This is a task from which no one can relieve us." And in his *Zeitschrift*, 1936, page 247, he exhorted the German people: "Do not be narrow-minded but think in large terms of great spaces, in continents and oceans, and thereby direct your course with that of your Führer."

The exhortation to acquire wide geographical information is wholly commendable. What brought Haushofer so near to the criminals' dock in the company of Ribbentrop was the admonition to "direct your course with that of your Führer," whom he described in another passage as a "God-given leader." This canonization of Hitler—which was frequent—is

---

* In his testimony before the International Military Tribunal for the Far East in December 1947 Prime Minister Tojo made frequent mention of Matsuoka's tendency toward drastic measures against the United States. Tojo described Matsuoka as being in frequent contact with Herr Stahmer, Nazi Ambassador to Tokyo during the period preceding Pearl Harbor. It was this uncompromising attitude of Matsuoka that led to the resignation of the second Konoye Cabinet and forced Matsuoka out of office.

in flat contradiction to Haushofer's statement during the Nuremberg interrogations that he never described Hitler as Führer but only as "tribune." His widely read booklet, *National Socialist Thought in the World* (1933), was a glorification of the Hitler regime and a plea for its extension on an international basis. In his *Geopolitics of the Pacific Ocean* he has a bitter passage to the effect that "only the destruction and decomposition" of the Versailles powers can guarantee life for Germany (1924, page 162). In his *Journal of Geopolitics*, 1930, page 961, he presents what is a virtual recommendation for Japan to relieve her population pressure by expanding into a sphere of least resistance and subtly draws her attention to Australia.

We have already seen that in his book *Wehr-Geopolitik* (Geopolitics of War), republished after the outbreak of hostilities, Haushofer has a chapter entitled "*Geopolitics of the Liberation War of the Axis Powers*." It is, as I had pointed out to him at Nuremberg, in effect a eulogy of the tactics and objectives of the Nazi armed forces. This approbation of the aggressive war policy of the Nazis was brought forcibly to his attention during the interrogation of October 6, 1945, when I asked him if he acknowledged the correctness of my translation of that chapter. It will be remembered that he replied: "Your views regarding this chapter, I, unfortunately, have to say are quite correct. At that time I really had the intention to end my life, but I have to say that because of my wife and the five children which she had brought into the world and the threat that was over her to be sent to Theresienstadt, I could not follow such a course....You are quite right. This is very difficult for me to say."

In making this painful admission, Haushofer displayed the same self-castigating psychology that another German witness manifested in open court at Nuremberg. On January 7, 1946, General Erich von dem Bach Zelewsky, an SS general who had decided to tell the entire truth, added, after one difficult admission: "It is hard for a German to force himself to this conclusion. It required much effort to do it." The expressive

German verb *durchzuringen* was used, i.e., "to wrestle with oneself—to battle one's way through."

Von dem Bach Zelewsky's testimony referred to his activities as commanding general of a special SS contingent operating on the Eastern Front against partisans. Himmler had given instructions that the Slavic population of eastern Europe should be "reduced by 30 per cent"—which gave wide latitude to experienced murderers and past masters of collective extermination. Asked if this directive represented Himmler's private beliefs, or did it form part of a settled and official policy, Von dem Bach Zelewsky replied that it was an inevitable consequence of National Socialist teaching which regarded Slavs as an inferior race and considered Jews as not men at all. Such teaching, spread over so many years, could only result, he said, in a final explosion. When this forthright witness left the stand and was passing by the prisoner's dock, Reichsmarshal Göring hissed at him: "Pig dog and traitor."

The ruthless application of such a policy and of Haushofer's thesis that small nations have no right to exist have given rise to a new word in international law and relations: *genocide*. Formed by a combination of the Greek word for race and the Latin word for murder, it was invented by my distinguished colleague at Nuremberg, Professor Raphael Lemkin of Duke University; it extends the concept awakened by terms such as homicide, fratricide, and matricide, to embrace the crime of murdering a whole nation. In pursuance of genocide, the Nazi policy in Poland was not a process of Germanizing a conquered province but, with organized technique, of applying unbelievable measures of biological, cultural, and religious extermination. In the language of the British chief prosecutor at Nuremberg: "Mass murder was becoming a state industry with byproducts."

The Nazi program in Poland struck at the roots of that people's vitality and racial continuity by decrees postponing the age of marriage for Poles, by sterilization of selected specimens of Polish manhood, by deporting others as slaves to Germany, by execution or imprisonment of intellectual leaders, by persecution of religion, by suffocating national art, education, legal institutions, and similar expressions of the characteristic genius of a race. Mass murder was practiced, to be sure, by the Nazis against their own people, but with a difference. At home they struck savagely at what they called political opposition. There was no thought of weakening the Germanic nation as a racial entity, but, allegedly, their elimination of domestic opponents was to strengthen and purify the Nordic stock. There was no connotation of undercutting the roots of biological fertility or cultural growth. It was this new and ghastly motivation in the administration of conquered territories that induced Winston Churchill to say in a radio address in August 1941: "...we are in the presence of a crime without a name," and caused Pius XII to protest to the German Foreign Office on October 8, 1942, against decrees and ordinances "at variance with the natural law and with the dispositions accepted by the legal systems of all nations."

The term genocide was employed in the indictment delivered to the twenty-one major Nazi criminals in October 1945, and the concept was publicly developed by the British prosecutor, Sir Hartley Shawcross, in his summation for the British Government at Nuremberg on July 26, 1946. Later, at the New York meeting of the United Nations' Assembly, Sir Hartley recommended that the term be incorporated in the law of nations—a proposal which was unanimously accepted by the Legal Committee of the United Nations' General Assembly on December 9, 1946. It is because of the untiring and scholarly labor of Professor Lemkin that the expression is included in the vocabulary of international criminality—though one may hope only as historical notation of a crime which never again can be tolerated by the conscience of humanity. Though, doubtless, genocide was never consciously intended by Karl Haushofer, it was implicit in much of his teachings, given the ruthless and amoral instincts of the ruling clique to whom he proffered such advice as the abhorrent principle that small nations have no right to exist in a modern world, or that German political power should follow on the heels of German cultural advance.

"Geopolitics is the duty to safeguard the right to the soil, to the land in the widest sense, not only the land within the frontiers of the Reich, but the right to the more extensive folk and cultural lands." (*Zeitschrift für Geopolitik*, 1935, No. 12, pp. 443-48.)

Paul Schmidt, Hitler's gifted interpreter and associate of all his secrets, testified at Nuremberg: "The general objectives of the Nazi leadership were apparent from the start; namely, the domination of the European continent, to be achieved first by the incorporation of all German-speaking groups in the Reich, and second by territorial expansion under the slogan of *Lebensraum*."

Hitler himself made use of this central Haushofer doctrine, as we learn from a document from the German Naval Archives. On the occasion of conversations held at the Führer's Headquarters between the ninth and eleventh of August 1943, Hitler declared to his naval advisers: "Only if all of Europe is united under a strong central power can there be any security for Europe from now on. Small sovereign states no longer have a right to exist." This revealing document, captured at Tambach, ends with a notation signed by Admiral Doenitz, Commander in Chief of the Nazi Navy:

> "The enormous stength which the Führer radiates, his unwavering confidence, and his farsighted appraisal of the Italian situation, have made it very clear in these days that we are all very insignificant in comparison with the Führer....Anyone who believes he can do better than the Führer is silly."

Unfortunately, the geographic materialism and determination of Haushofer's geopolitics were supplemented by a concomitant rationalization in the field of law and jurisprudence. The world of letters soon beheld another illegitimate progeny come to birth: *geojurisprudenz*, which deformed and restricted the concept of law and equity by geographic considerations. Instead of a universal law of nations we saw international justice defined in terms of exclusive national utility unilaterally defined. Thus, corruption of the *jus gentium*, or law of nations, was aptly summarized by Frank, Nazi Minister of Justice, at the Congress of German Jurists, at Leipzig, October 2-5, 1935, when he said: "*Recht ist was dem deutschen Volk nützt und unrecht was ihm schadet* [Justice means whatever is useful to the German people and injustice whatever harms them]." Legality became a geographical concept. And, worse still, as we shall find in a later chapter, we had the distortions of jurisprudence popularized by Karl Schmitt from the University of Berlin.

These evil consequences of false geopolitics and its concomitant provocations must not blind us to the power for good in a true geopolitics. Is there such a thing as legitimate geopolitics? Assuredly, yes. I have conducted courses on that subject for many years at Georgetown University and at army schools for the training of staff and commanding officers. Germany itself once had an excellent tradition of sound geographical research. Alexander von Humboldt was, it may be truly said, the father of modern geography, and I know of few maps better than those once produced by the house of Justus Perthes, at Gotha. Humboldt ranged the world from Siberia to South America, and his findings on the relationship existing between man and his environment were copious, minute, and scientific. His encyclopedic work, *Cosmos*, is known to every informed geographer. But Humboldt never turned his findings into an argument for physical aggression or power politics. It was the deadly sin of Karl Haushofer's geopolitics and the tragedy of his intellectual life that he took Machiavelli, not Humboldt, as master of his geographical conscience.

What did Haushofer add to previous exponents of human geography? Universality, practicality, and definite political objectives. He went far beyond the regional and limited scope of his classic predecessors in that field and became global; he discarded objectivity for subjective prejudices and interpreted geographic phenomena mainly in their relationship to the interests of Germany, thereby committing treason against that very scientific credo which Germany has so noisily worshiped as her outstanding creation. He first committed intellectual suicide on the altar of a vulgar and unscientific superstition, and ended with physical self-murder in a gully at Hartschimmelhof.

What did Hitler add to Haushofer's geopolitical trickery? Action, striking power, the will to end the long symposium and begin the indicated conquests. Conviction of Germanic destiny had been planted in his consciousness from long brooding over the doctrines of Gobineau, Fichte, Hegel, Treitschke, Nietzsche, Houston Stewart Chamberlain, Rosenberg, and similar messianic preachers of Teutonic superiority. That fixed idea exhausted the capacity of his brain and his soul; he chose the way of power above the way of law and reason.

But the excesses and brutalities which ensued must not obscure the residue of validity in the premises. On the basis of sound factual knowledge, the nations of the world must come to a reasonable and humane solution of boundary problems and to an equitable distribution of the fruits of the earth. Mutual respect, mutual understanding, mutual confidence must prevail or else mutual hatred, mutual suspicion, and the inevitable destruction of our civilization will ensue. Reasonable provision must be made for outlets in the case of countries of rapidly increasing population. When additional space for necessary emigration is honestly needed, when the pressure is authentic and natural, not alleged or artificial, negotiations should ensue before some competent tribunal with compensation and protection guaranteed to the conceding power. Otherwise brute force and the hysteria of peoples propagandized into a conviction of injury will again plunge the world into reciprocal slaughter and atomic chaos. A more equitable access to and control of essential raw materials in the world must, moreover, replace the virtual monopoly previously exercised by the favored few. Narrow exploitation of the rarer but necessary ingredients of modern industrial production which are found by accident of nature within the jurisdiction of America, England, Japan, Russia, China, Canada, or Bolivia can no longer be reconciled with the economic liberalism now assumed as the cornerstone of international peace. It will be futile to control atomic energy without first disciplining and spiritualizing the will and the intellect and the conscience of explosive human atoms.

Happily, in the field of law a newer concept of justice is beginning to breathe its vitalizing spirit through the halls of German universities. In the inaugural address of the first postwar rector of the university at Frankfurt-on-Main, who is a returned prisoner of war from the United States, certain expressions occur which will find welcome echo in the tired hearts of all men of good will; for there we read affirmations of the dignity of human personality, and indications of the moral, not the purely utilitarian basis of law. The election of Professor Hallstein by his German colleagues to preside over the reopened University of Frankfurt is one of the many encouraging results of the special project for reorienting German prisoners of war during their sojourn in the United States—that farsighted program initiated by General Bryan, the provost marshal, and initially administered by Colonel Wessels and Major Kraus in Germany. From the purification of private law, with which Dr. Hallstein's address was primarily concerned, to the rehabilitation of public law is a logical and an imperative step. From such beginnings can emerge the moral renaissance of Germany and the return of the German people to the full dignity of their better qualities.

The Government of the United States has never indicated or denounced the population of Germany as a whole, and Mr. Justice Jackson in his opening address on November 21, 1945, at Nuremberg, made it perfectly clear that the German people were not on trial before the International Military Tribunal. What was on trial was a specific group of designated individuals who had misused the German Government and the German people for criminal purposes. So, too, Pius XII, in his address to the College of Cardinals on June 2,

1945, clearly formulated the moral judgment of Christianity in the hour of Allied victory: "For over twelve years, twelve of the best years of our mature age, we had lived in the midst of the German people, fulfilling the duties of the office committed to us....We thus had occasion to learn the great qualities of that people and we were personally in close contact with its most representative men. For that reason we cherish the hope that it can rise to new dignity and new life when once it has laid the satanic specter raised by National Socialism and the guilty (as we have already at other times had occasion to expound) have expiated the crimes they have committed."

7. Russian Geopolitics and the United States

At a time when the Soviet Union had tested an atomic bomb, Great Britain developed a nuclear device and the United States was about to detonate the first thermonuclear weapon, Soviet-American relations had indeed deteriorated to an alarming level. Notwithstanding truce negotiations in the summer of 1951, the Korean war continued to rage, with both sides suffering casualties.

Father Walsh, in his typically informal style, recalled the conduct of foreign affairs by the Soviets and advanced his hypothesis that the Kremlin had adapted Haushofer's theory of the heartland to their own purposes, adding it to their own theories of world domination.

This was one of Father Walsh's last public addresses. In November, 1952, following a dinner celebrating his Golden Jubilee as a Jesuit, which was sponsored by the Georgetown Club of Washington, D.C., he suffered a stroke that made an invalid of him for the rest of his life.

May I at the outset express again, as I have had the privilege of doing over many, many years, the feeling of gratification and of service which I entertain in being permitted from year to year to be associated with the important work upon which you are engaged and with which you are concerned.

If I may be allowed to reminisce—I had the honor of lecturing to the Industrial War College, as it was then called, when, as I recollect, down in the old Munitions Building, it was not much more than a couple of offices and an auditorium; respectfully called an auditorium, probably achieved by knocking out the wall between two offices. Across the intervening years, the importance of the element that it emphasizes has become more and more apparent. Each year that I have had the privilege of lecturing, I have found a topic readily available. There has been one government on the face of the earth that has very benignly supplied me with subject matter since November 7, 1917. By the by, as I look around here, I remember that one of my earliest lectures before the War College was attended by a young captain by the name of Eisenhower, who became a major very shortly thereafter and subsequently enjoyed an astronomic rise in his career.

Each time I begin these discussions, despite what has happened in the meantime, I feel very much like a professor of the old, imperturbable German type who taught at the University of Innsbruck in Austria, which I attended in 1914. At some time during his career as a German lecturer there,

---

Lecture presented to the Industrial College of the Armed Forces, Washington, D.C. on August 26, 1952.

he was imprisoned by the Prussian Government because he dared to question some of the infallibilities that resided in that seat of wisdom. When he returned to begin his lectures again, the student body and all the faculty were, of course, assembled in numbers to see what the old gentleman would say, whether he would launch into an indictment or defense. But all he did was put on his specs, look at his audience and state: "Meine Herren, as I was saying when I was interrupted..."

Similarly, I should like to say that it would indeed be a very profitable prelude to any discussion of the United States' position and policy vis-à-vis Soviet Russia to trace the course of those relationships since November 7, 1917, as there is an organic continuity which requires a knowledge of the whole picture. This might possibly be done in two fat volumes running to about a thousand pages, but even such format would demand that the author have a special genius for selectivity, condensation and a very terse and disciplined style because of the vast amount of material at his disposal!

Therefore, I have to omit a great deal and must confine myself to a very limited discussion of an enormous and still growing field. I intend not only to speak of the physical and geographical facts of geopolitics, but also to discuss certain aspects of our present foreign policy as revealed in the diplomatic processes now "en marche".

First of all, I feel it a duty to emphasize before every class the fact that the underlying and permanent strategy of the Politburo has been persistent and consistent since 1917, though it often comes up with tactical changes and zigzags. Now, as these zigzags take place, particularly in Russia's diplomatic procedures, we experience a recurrence of optimism, that we are about to witness a drift to the right and, consequently, the possibility of co-existence. However, any maneuver of that kind is usually traceable to some setback in Russia's program or to some unforeseen shift in the overall balance of power....

Now, let us look at the present situation: The great gamble in Korea failed in its basic objective and a year of false armistice negotiations ensued, a respite welcomed as an opportunity to build up forces for the next assault, wherever it may be launched. And in Europe, the various political and economic devices have strengthened the resistance against the Kremlin: the Marshall Plan clearly had a beneficial effect on the economy, the North Atlantic Treaty Organization is being strengthened militarily, although not sufficiently, and the Schuman Plan has progressed satisfactorily. These measures have displaced the demoralization and fears we all saw in Europe during the first few years after the War.

You and I have noticed in recent days the spectacular announcement that Mr. Stalin has called a meeting of the Communist Party for October 5, at which important organizational and structural changes would be made. Now, that always means something more than appears on the surface. Those familiar with Soviet political zigzags and with Lenin's directions for such cases, clearly see that about this time a zigzag is indicated, unless the Politburo in desperation is ready to hazard a provocation that might tip the scale towards the ultimate horror of open warfare against the United States.

While I do not consider open warfare imminent, I do not propose to differ with an eminent military authority now engaged in the most hazardous battle of his whole life, who said recently that we were facing the greatest danger in the history of the Republic.

I have always maintained, Gentlemen, that the Russian Revolution of 1917 and all its consequences represented the most important single political event since the fall of the Roman Empire. I expounded that doctrine in this hall, and later in the other hall, at a time when people in high diplomatic and political echelons were saying "Don't you think this has got on your nerves, Father?" One high diplomatic officer once said to me: "Why not run down to Miami with me and we will bake it out on the sands?" I noticed in later years that they went farther south than Miami, even to Key West, to "bake it out."....

The notion that ultimate hostilities are inevitable has been clearly predicted in the statements of Lenin and Stalin. It is still the belief in Russia today, their basic dogma, which has never been repudiated. However, statements regarding potential hostilities are often toned down for tactical purposes in hours of danger.

Lenin set that pattern himself when he insisted upon signing that humiliating treaty of Brest-Litovsk in 1918, because his world revolution was endangered by the approach of the German army towards St. Petersburg. Later on, he did not hesitate to scrap integral communism in Russia itself. He restored private enterprise in the new economic policy of 1922, because Russia was faced with an appalling famine, as I witnessed during my stay there.

Next, the Marxist groups invaded the united front with democracy. They organized against nazism and fascism in 1935 because their sensitive revolutionary nose smelled the menace of a powerful competitor for the leadership for world revolution in the person of Adolf Hitler.

Subsequently, Stalin executed a diplomatic somersault and entered into partnership with Nazi Germany in 1939 when the wind began to blow from another direction. And that made World War II inevitable. Then he congratulated his fellow totalitarian on the rape of Poland. But when his Nazi bedfellow rolled over on him in 1941 and nearly suffocated him by invading Russia, the Politburo straightaway turned to the hated bourgeoisie of the West for aid, comfort and lend-lease. There need be no elucidation, I think, of what has happened since 1945. It must suffice to recall for my present purposes that once the Nazi menace was eliminated, Soviet foreign policy soon reverted to the unchanged partyline.

Because of indecision on our part, because of misconception of the issue, because of divided counsel, and, alas, because of too great confidence in Soviet pledges by certain quarters that should have known better, Western diplomacy was out-maneuvered and was checkmated in the game for international stakes, played with the greatest chess players of the world. I wish again to emphasize that I believe it a sterile approach to the problem if I were to make that incredible record of misunderstanding and overconfidence a sort of whipping post for recrimination and for the indictment of any personality or personalities. Therefore, I will refer to it only insofar as the costly errors of the past may serve as lamps to our feet in the future.

Above and beyond all contemporary statements and documents, above and beyond what happened at Teheran, Yalta and Potsdam, stands one indisputably malignant geographical fact, which ought to be kept before the minds of Republicans and Democrats alike, and which should be the target of their best marksmanship....

Let us look, then, to the facts. Seven years of study and planned conquest by the Soviets since 1945 have resulted in a new Communist Empire, the largest in recorded history. Some 800 million human beings are now, directly or indirectly, subjected to the control of the Kremlin; that means approximately one-third of the human race, and the end is not yet in sight. I saw some of this panorama unfolding under my own eyes in 1945 in Germany and later on in the Far East; it has evolved with foresight, forethought and geopolitical wisdom.

The reason why I often insist upon the last feature is because I have worked in the field of geopolitics for a good many years. As early as 1924, after my return from Russia, I began to notice a German magazine crossing my desk, called *Zeitschrift für Geopolitik*. It was then that I made my first contact with the remarkable figure that I later on interviewed at Nuremberg, namely General Karl Haushofer. From that highly intellectual magazine, particularly from the geographical discussions and the type of maps it contained, I realized that he was more than a conventional geographer. A dynamic force was at work, showing global perspective and promoting the slow building up of a philosophy of power for the German Government. And, you remember, that he adapted the famous, often cited statement of Sir Halford Mackinder which I consider one of the most brilliant hypotheses of modern political science, to the following:

"Who rules East Europe commands the Continent of Europe; who rules the Continent of Europe commands the Heartland and who rules the Heartland commands the world."

I do not intend to go into the particular aspect of geopolitics again, except to consider its impact; even Haushofer never realized the tragedy that was to follow.

Now, what have the Bolsheviks done, geographically? Either in your **mind's eye** or by concentration on a map, you will see that there are three great "power centers" in the world, I mean concentrations of countries which are distinctly recognizable for their economic resources, climate, and organizational advancement. The first, of course, is the European complex, which would run, say, from England over to Poland, and south as far as the Mediterranean. The second great power center is recognizable on the eastern end of the Heartland and would include Japan, China, Manchuria and Southeast Asia. This is an area which, though not as great as the western complex, is full of untapped resources which, if properly developed, could make it the leading world power. The third great reservoir of power is in the Atlantic world, mostly on the eastern borders of the United States and in southeastern Canada.

You will note that Western Europe is threatened by Soviet power and the Asian complex is in part occupied by Soviet power. The only untouched but threatened reservoir is the Atlantic region. That concept, I think, has led to the next developments. Whereas Mackinder and Haushofer would say "Who controls East Europe commands the Heartland..." and so on, I think the Russians are saying now that who controls the rimlands, the borders of Europe and Asia, can protect the heartland of the World Revolution. The desired objective has been the rule of the rimlands, in order to provide bases for the erection of offensive and defensive installations for the protection of the heartland and to serve as springboard for whatever lies in the obscure future. That, I think, is the geographic scheme. We all know the political and social patterns.

Now, that is merely a hypothesis of mine, but if you treat it like an overlay in the laboratory and place it over the landscape, you see how far our supposition touches the actualities of the map. The Russians control, of course, the northern shore of their own country and lay claim to about 50 per cent of all the offshore territory within the Arctic Circle. And we know what is going on in these regions: the feverish activity in northern Siberia of building new airfields and a great push toward Kamchatka and the coast of Alaska; the army and the defense installations in general have retreated from some of the furthermost points of the Aleutians to a region that is more defensible. On the coast of China they control all of Sakhalin and the Kuriles, which were handed to them on a platter. In Europe, they control Pechenka or Petsamo in the North of Finland and aim at the Adriatic ports, but always excluding Yugoslavia, to be repossessed when they think it advisable to do so. They also tried to make Greece an eastern anchor of their power, but the implementation of the Truman Doctrine frustrated their plans. After Greece, the next targets would have been Gibraltar and Spain, as western anchors of their power, enabling them to control the entire Mediterranean. These are frequently mentioned objectives. That is why they were so annoyed at Franco, as Spain was a test case in the course of 1935. They were there because they knew that once a revolution would be started, only a Soviet form of government was the natural, and in their opinion, inevitable form of government to emerge. They would then have practically bracketed Europe and Asia, all in accordance with this rimland hypothesis.

This particular geographic development, in my opinion, does not represent Marxian theory but rather a Germanic ideology. I have not the slightest doubt that there are members of the old Haushofer School in Russia today as well as technical experts in the scientific field. But we have nothing to complain about in that respect, because I think we took a few ourselves. I believe that we have the top drawer with respect to the atomic process, because of that infusion of new blood just before and after the cessation of hostilities.

Another point to remember, which is amusing to me, relates to the Soviet Union's demand on Ecuador for fishing rights off the Galapagos Islands. Fishing rights for the country that has the greatest maritime fishing backyard on the face of the earth! It is clear that the fish they wanted were swimming in the Panama canal! And, as you may also know, they demanded a protectorate in Libya, which was turned down by the United Nations.

You have to watch each geographical move the Soviets make; they are all connected and add up to something like the hypothesis of Mackinder but changing the importance of the heartland to that of the rimlands. I reiterate my belief that the possession of the rimlands for recognizable purposes constitutes their present policy. Alas, how wonderfully they have succeeded!

In terms of space and geography, nearly 300,000 square miles have fallen to the new Ghengis Khan in Europe, with several millions added to his garrison in Asia. A study of the map will clarify Soviet Russia's new geopolitical position. Her strategic boundaries are no longer lines on a map, but peripheral zones of power in Asia and Europe to be constantly pushed outward from Moscow, thus providing both depth for the defense of the center of the heartland and forward bases for offensive installations.

The circumstances, which the Russians faced with extreme realism after 1945, required a new type of diplomacy and of international relations. International peace through international negotiations formed the hard core of the art of diplomacy in past generations. Mutuality, reciprocity and respect for international law were assumed. But these premises never existed in the political philosophy of your Marxian diplomats, as they consider themselves agents of a world government, of a world revolution rather than representatives of one government. They were ordained to the apostolate of universal domination by one privileged group. Their ultimate reliance is on the diplomacy of power, not on the power of traditional diplomacy. Soviet diplomats are not negotiators; they are trained revolutionists assigned to the office of special services in the camp of the Philistines.

...It is indeed gratifying to observe a gradual realization of that cold reality in the minds of our present policy makers. However, why the obvious was so long suppressed, or at least minimized, remains a closely guarded secret. I remember once discussing with President Roosevelt the matter of international relations and our fundamental differences regarding the U.S. position toward the Soviet Union. Nevertheless, he extended to me the courtesy of calling me to the White House in 1933 on the very day when he officially recognized Soviet Russia. "I want you to know what I am doing today," he said. "Now, Father Walsh, I realize that you have opposed this, but leave it to me, I am a good horsetrader." Well, you and I have seen the spavined nag that he acquired!

Today, however, you and I are observing a welcome realism slowly evolving into concrete measures. The international comity and the practice of international law have always recognized the validity of actions other than war, such as repression, retaliation, and even blockades. Cautiously, but surely, I think, American policy is now exercising its rights, in the proper manner, by imposing on Soviet officials and diplomats certain pressures that have long been employed against our and all other foreign representatives in the Soviet Union. Consequently, our State Department now limits the physical movements of Soviet and satellite diplomats; it forbids them to travel without permission beyond a specified distance from Washington, as the Kremlin has been controlling the travels of American officials in the Soviet Union. However, the Soviets have one unique advantage: they still have the United Nations available for the placement of their agents who enjoy there full freedom to travel to any place in the United States. The virtual strangulation of *Amerika*, the publication sponsored by this Government in Russia, has, as you know, been countered by the discontinuance of the *Bulletin of Information* which the Soviet Embassy had available in Washington, D.C. These mild assertions of reciprocity, and I have enumerated only a few, are instantly understood at Moscow, where only power is respected. The state of rearmament of America and Europe, with American assistance, is a form of diplomatic development immensely adapted to the cold war that has been waged against the United States since the beginning of the Russian Revolution.

The normal functions of our ambassador to Moscow have been substantially curtailed under conditions deliberately created by the Kremlin; hence, the new diplomacy of power, getting up our courage and talking in monosyllables to the Soviet Union. That, of course, is a late development, but the only practical measures which they understand. It is an historically necessary substitute for what they have abolished in the world, namely, reciprocal confidence and respect for international law. President Truman's recent visit to New Haven for the ceremonies regarding the laying of the keel of our first submarine to be powered by atomic energy was worth a dozen unnecessary odd memoranda, and the work already begun on the giant aircraft carrier "Forrestal" has needed no clarification whatsoever for the boys in the Kremlin.

Part IV

Is It Immoral to Strike First?

With General Douglas MacArthur during E.A. Walsh's visit to Tokyo in 1947.

8. Is It Immoral to Strike First If Attack Is Imminent?

At a time when the cold war threatened to break into open hostilities in Korea, the potential use of atomic weapons posed both a military and a moral dilemma to political leaders. The United States had used this frightful weapon to end Japan's resistance in World War II, but without fear of retaliation, as at that time Germany had been defeated and, to common knowledge, Japan did not have the bomb. By the end of 1950, the situation had changed, as the Soviet Union reportedly had the capability to produce atomic weapons.

Father Walsh believed that the United States would be justified in taking any defensive measures, including the use of the atom bomb before an actual attack by the Soviet Union, if our leaders were certain that a surprise attack was indeed imminent. In his book *Total Empire*, Father Walsh elaborated on the United States' responsibility to use atomic weapons to defend herself. Furthermore, as the United States had accepted the principle of collectively guaranteeing the security of any United Nations member, the use of the atom bomb against an aggressor recognized by the United Nations, even if the attack was not directed against the United States, would not violate Christian morality. "The debate is not whether we can afford to do the necessary things for the defense of Christian civilization, but can we afford not to do them." This, he believed, was the problem which faced the

American people and their leaders. It is the latter issue that Father Walsh addressed in this article, which preceded publication of *Total Empire*. Published in 1951, the book was a best-seller and earned Father Walsh the Golden Book Award of the Catholic Writers Guild of America in the following year.

Father Walsh's views on the use of the atom bomb generated strong reaction in his time and the problem of ethics in national defense still represents a central issue in Catholic social teaching.

The President's proclamation of December 16, 1950, declaring a state of national emergency in response to the events in Korea, marked the end of what is probably the most amazing and confused chapter in the history of American foreign policy. The official description and recognition of the objectives of world communism by the Presidential decree put the issue, at long last, exactly where it belongs. The final confrontation has been reached between the two great centers of world power whose basic and irreconcilable character was frankly described by Soviet authorities many years ago. They never had a moment's doubt as to the inevitable clash that must ensue. Lenin knew it and warned his followers:

> "We live...not only in a state but in a system of states, and the existence of the Soviet Republic side by side with the imperialist states [i.e., non-communist states] for a long time is unthinkable. In the end either one or the other will conquer. And until that end comes, a series of the most terrible collisions between the Soviet Republic and the bourgeois states is inevitable."

After citing this fundamental Soviet doctrine, Stalin once added the laconic remark: "Clear, one would think."

In 1927, he likewise declared to a visiting delegation of American workers:

> "Thus in the course of further development of international revolution, two centers will form on a world

---

Article in *The Sunday Star*, Washington, D.C., December 24, 1950.

scale...The struggle of these two centers for the possession of the world economy will decide the fate of capitalism and communism in the whole world."

The hard core, the stronghold and arsenal of the non-communist forces in this conflict with Soviet communism are the United States—a diagnosis which Mr. Stalin confirmed in his interview with former Governor Stassen in 1947. Neither he [Stalin] nor any Leninist believes in the continued coexistence of these two opposing worlds of economic thought and moral ideals. The protestations of peaceful intent spoken by Mr. Vishinsky in the United Nations are only the actor's lines of a prepared script designed to distract the audience from an approaching Pearl Harbor.

It is for that inevitable, titanic Armageddon that Soviet rearmament has been in preparation since 1945. There is, consequently, a recognizable logicality in Soviet maneuvers, whether on the diplomatic front or in their territorial aggrandizements, which makes Soviet conduct coldly consistent and not an enigma, or a puzzle, as some unhistoric minds imagine. The Politburo has ordered many a zigzag, to be sure, but their overall strategy reveals the most coherent national policy and effective staff planning observable on the stage of international relations for the past 30 years. Look at a map of the world: something like 800 million human beings are now directly or indirectly under the control of Moscow, approximately one-third of the human race.

The place of A-bombs and H-bombs in this complex clash of power between East and West is, like the ghost of Banquo, the uninvited guest at every international conference. Ready to scrap the advantage conferred by those ghastly weapons if all other nations would agree to effective controls, the Government of the United States has been blocked by the constant veto of Soviet Russia. Thus she gains time while the sands run out—till she has a stockpile of atomic bombs. Hence, regretfully but categorically, President Truman announced on April 6, 1949, that he would authorize the use of atomic bombs again, should the dreaded necessity arise and if the welfare of the United States and the democracies of the world are at stake. "I hope and pray," he added, "that will never be necessary."

The frightful effects of the dreadful weapon are known by personal observation to this writer, as he spent some ten days in the ruins of Hiroshima in 1947 and interviewed many of the victims who survived the tragedy. The ethical problem of employing such a lethal weapon which, by the very nature and intensity of the explosion will exterminate thousands upon thousands of civilians and innocent bystanders not directly employed in military activities, is not easy to resolve. Discussion of that moral aspect is made intricate and inconclusive, moreover, by the new and inescapable fact of total warfare.

The degeneration in international conduct since 1939 and the evil of total war have produced profound public consequences. There is no longer a battlefront in the conventional sense; there is no longer a defined and limited zone of combat occupied by military forces, by men who are expected to run the risks of soldiers, leaving a rear territory inhabited by civilians not subject to the same hazards under the old concept of warfare. Today the total population is involved; the needs of technological developments embrace so much organization for armament and for supply that the battle front has moved into every city, town and village. There is no rear; there is no escape; and there is no shield of legal status. What is of immediate concern, then, is definition and clarification of the issue raised by President Truman's reference to necessity and the welfare of the United States, followed by his authorization to proceed with production of the hydrogen bomb.

Direct assault launched against us by an enemy who is known to have the atomic bomb—and no power would now attack the United States without it—raises one type of question which is not too difficult to answer. We should have no alternative but to retaliate in kind. A second question is more compelling and it is with this that we are here concerned: Would the United States be justified in launching an immediate atomic attack against an enemy power before it could use that devastating weapon against our cities? Under any hypothesis, the answer is extremely difficult to formulate, both for ethical and historical reasons. Our every tradition and instinct as a people, as well as our conscience, recoil before such a dreadful alternative even in self-defense, although few moralists will insist that we must wait until the enemy delivers the first atomic blow. Under the new conditions of the atomic age such an aggression might very well be fatal, not only to a vast number of individuals, as is obvious, but also to our entire system of national defense and to our existence as a Nation. Clearly, atomic bombs would be used under the title of defense only, a claim that would be set up by every nation. Hence, the concept and term "defense" must be clarified, both by definition and through application to concrete circumstances.

The use of force for legitimate self-defense is conferred by natural law. This moral justification to repel an unjust aggressor by means reasonably adapted and proportionate to the nature of the attack, is the right not only of individuals but of the state as well. In the case of the state, it goes further still; it becomes an obligation, in view of the duty incumbent on government to safeguard the lives, the liberty and the temporal welfare of citizens viewed individually and collectively. In total war the attack is no longer limited to acknowledged military targets; it is leveled against whole peoples.

The problem, then, involves questions relating to the certainty and immediacy of an attack under given circumstances as well as to the special nature of some new defensive weapon. In the evolution of human relationships from primitive to modern and complex, the elements of certainty and immediacy have varied in step with the development of weapons of attack. Primitive man was justified in exercising his right to strike a preventive blow when he saw a bare fist descending on him at arm's length, or a stone lifted against him. In the course of time he saw an ax uplifted, a dagger drawn, a sword thrust at him, then a spear leveled, then an arrow fitted to a bowstring. The danger, though moving back in space, was still immediate and certain in time. With the invention of gunpowder, the assailant moved farther and farther away; but no basic change was introduced in the elements of certainty and immediacy of attack. Later on, long-range artillery, though discharging explosives from emplacements even out of sight and miles away, could menace life and limb with equal certainty and immediacy.

Now comes the age of air power, with military aviation carrying flaming death from bases located up to 5,000 miles away. Aircraft carriers far out at sea, flying bombs, guided missiles, jet bombs and atomic explosives can now be a certain and immediate menace from evergrowing distances in this era of globalminded warfare. Who shall maintain that the substantive and inherent right of self-defense is cancelled out by an accidental circumstance or by the ingenuity of an aggressor in a chemical laboratory?

The Japanese air force which bombed Pearl Harbor was carried to a point designated for the take-off by a fleet of war vessels, including carriers, which, we now know, left the northern Japanese port of Tankan Wan on November 26, 1941, for the attack delivered on December 7. The attacking planes took off from the decks of their carriers at a point approximately 230 miles north of Pearl Harbor. It would be a tortured interpretation of the right of self-defense to deny the corresponding right to have intercepted and destroyed that advancing menace at any point, near or far.

Should history repeat itself and produce a Soviet feint in some remote area of Asia or the Middle East, it will be the signal for those burnt once in the fire of such deceit to keep their eyes fixed on the Northwest and Arctic sector of our American defense system.

If the Government of the United States has sound reason to believe (that is, has moral certitude) that a similar attack is being mounted and ready to be launched against this country from any source, then it would appear that President Truman would be morally justified to take defensive measures proportionate to the danger. That would mean use of the atomic bomb, as no power would launch a surprise attack on the United States without an adequate supply of atomic bombs. Should large numbers of civilians be harmed by American necessity to use the bomb in self-defense, that regrettable effect, not intended as such, would be attributable to what moralists describe as the indirect voluntary. An attack against us would have to be sudden, unannounced, sufficiently devastating and so widespread in coverage as to cripple our powers of reprisal; the reply to any partial crippling would be so overwhelmingly atomic that no aggressive government could risk the gamble without certainty of success. Losing the gamble under present conditions of warfare would mean practical annihilation.

This argument presupposes, as its crucial premise, accuracy of information, honest information, competent information, and an alert intelligence service. If time permitted, a warning or an ultimatum to an enemy found to be preparing such an attack should be given. But, with or without ultimatum, I personally see no immorality, though much tragedy and horror of consequences, in the Government of the United States choosing the lesser of two evils. Neither reason nor theology, nor morals require men or nations to commit suicide by prescribing that people must await the first blow from a power with no moral inhibitions and when, as in the case now under consideration, the attack would surely include bombardment by atomic missiles.

Even Christ himself did not disdain to seize a lash and drive the hypocrites out of the Temple. What an appalling responsibility is now laid on military intelligence, on diplomatic vigilance and on all related security agencies which gather and analyze information in this atomic age.

PART V

IN HONOR OF GREAT MEN

Father E.A. Walsh, S.J. enjoying the accolades of friends and admirers at his Golden Jubilee celebration. To the right of toastmaster Benjamin M. McKelway, editor, the *Evening Star:* Father E.A. Walsh, S.J.; His Excellency, the Most Rev. Amleto Giovanni Cicognani, Apostolic Delegate to the United States; the Hon. Willard L. Beaulac, U.S. ambassador to Cuba, one of the first graduates of the School of Foreign Service; Rabbi Norman Gerstenfeld, minister, Washington Hebrew Congregation. To the toastmaster's left: His Excellency, the Most Rev. Patrick A. O'Boyle, archbishop of Washington, D.C.; Gen. J. Lawton Collins, chief of staff, U.S. Army; the Very Rev. Edward B. Bunn, S.J., president, Georgetown University; Hon. Charles Fahy, circuit judge, U.S. Court of Appeals for the District of Columbia.

9. A Sermon from a Stained Glass Window

On May 19, 1892, "with imposing ceremonies in the presence of a distinguished company of prelates," led by James Cardinal Gibbons, the cornerstone was laid for the Chapel of the Sacred Heart on the west side of the quadrangle behind the Healy Building. The chapel was built through the munificence of Mr. John V. Dahlgren, an alumnus graduated in 1891, and his wife, in memory of their son who had died in infancy. Both he and members of his family are buried in the crypt under the altar. It was the first structure on campus which was named after a non-Jesuit.

The outstanding features of the English gothic building are the stained glass windows portraying the saints who were chosen as patrons of the students. One of these windows depicts Sir Thomas More, the chancellor of Henry VIII, who died "the King's good servant, but God's first."

It was in this chapel that Father Walsh delivered a memorial sermon at a sodality meeting of Foreign Service School students while, simultaneously, the canonization ceremonies of Sir Thomas More and Bishop John Fisher were transmitted to the world by radio from the Vatican.

Today, at this very hour, in the Eternal City, a ceremony is being enacted which puts the Church's ultimate seal of sanctity on one of the most distinguished laymen of the Catholic Church, Sir Thomas More, the great Chancellor of England under Henry VIII. At the same time, a saintly Bishop and Cardinal, John Fisher, Bishop of Rochester, is also being elevated to the aureole of sainthood. But it is to the significance of Sir Thomas More's life that I would draw your attention today, as he may well be considered the patron and most shining example for every Catholic layman.

For many years, in anticipation of this day, his revered figure has been in this chapel, pictured there in the last stained glass window on the gospel side.

The scene that is taking place in St. Peter's Basilica today has a particular significance in that it is a reminder of the ancient conflict that has raged immemorially on the stage of human affairs. The four hundred years that have elapsed since Thomas More said "no" to Henry VIII have reproduced the same conflict in changed circumstances and under forms of accidental variety, but the main issue was ever the same. In More's case the problem was accentuated and became the focal point of interest to all Christendom because the protagonists were world figures; one a powerful King, the other the Chief Legal Officer of England, Henry's own choice for Chancellor.

The issue was clean cut. Here was a favorite counselor of the King who had risen rapidly to universal esteem by the integrity of his character, the purity of his life and the

---

Homily given at Dahlgren Chapel, Georgetown University, on May 19, 1935.

brilliance of his intellect. More was one of that group of intellectual princes whose genius made the Renaissance. Author of the first and most famous *Utopia*, intimate of Erasmus of Rotterdam and peer of the most brilliant scholars of Europe, he received a long line of well merited honors from his King and country: Privy Counselor, Under-Treasurer of the Realm, Speaker of the House of Commons, Ambassador to foreign lands, High Steward of Cambridge University, Under-Sheriff of London and, finally, Chancellor of England, the first lay lawyer ever to hold that post and to share almost equal power with the King.

But the tragic schism that was to rend Christendom in twain and set brother against brother, father against son, and turn innocent children into hated informers, was not long in reaching England. The King would divorce his legitimate wife, Catherine of Aragon, declare himself Head of the Church and master of the spiritual as well as the temporal life of his subjects. A subservient Parliament succumbed to the royal whim. While lesser hearts grew faint and heads began to fall, More and Fisher remained unshaken in head and heart. To all the attractive arguments this world can muster, long life, honor, riches, country estates and town houses, power and influence, they returned the same answer that the Christians in the Colosseum gave to Nero: "We cannot and we will not put any man's favor above the law of God." Willingly and properly admitting the King's supreme temporal power as monarch of the land to whom unquestioned civil loyalty was due, More rendered unto Caesar the things that are Caesar's, but refused to Caesar the things that are God's. In return, he underwent a long, miserable imprisonment in the Tower, which culminated in his execution by beheading on July 6, 1535. His bleeding head was affixed to London Bridge for 30 days.

The first and tenderest tribute to More was written by a fellow Englishman, not of the Catholic faith. Joseph Addison, in number 349 of the *Spectator* of April 10, 1712 wrote:

"...That innocent Mirth, which had been so conspicuous in his Life did not forsake him to the last..his Death was of a piece with his Life. There was nothing in it new, forced or affected. He did not look upon the severing of his Head from his Body as a Circumstance that ought to produce any Change in the disposition of his Mind..."

The wheel of time has turned relentlessly for four centuries and today the martyr's crown has been acknowledged by solemn acclamation of all men, friend and foe alike. But the lapse of centuries has also brought a return of the identical conflict between Caeasar and conscience. The old, old combat is again being fought in Russia, Mexico and Germany. It will recur tomorrow and after, so long as human passions clash with conscience. Who will say that it will not come to you or me in the United States? We are not immune. The day may not be far off when the Catholic Church in America will be the last bulwark against rampant materialism, arrogant nationalism and international atheism sponsored by the Mongolian satraps in Moscow. There are even some who think that they already detect the first signs of such a conflict between the individual and the state.

It is not my function to discuss from this altar those specific problems at the present time. But it is my function to remind ourselves that, should they arise, we are to draw our strength, our solace and our light from that same resource which illuminated Thomas More. Even as Chancellor, morning after morning, he would don the garb of an acolyte and reverently serve the altar. The Duke of Norfolk once remonstrated: "What? You a parish altarboy! You dishonor the King and his great office." "Nay," replied Sir Thomas, smiling as he always did, "It cannot be displeasing to my Lord the King, that I pay homage to the King's Lord."

He followed his conscience to the very foot of the scaffold. He mounted the ladder, rung by rung, with fortitude, charity and serenity, for he knew it was the path to that eternal truth to which Simon Peter so generously confessed one morning on the shore of the lake:

"Thou art the Christ, the Son of the Living God. Thou hast the words of eternal life. If we leave Thee, to whom shall we go?"

President Dwight D. Eisenhower, unveiling the bust of Father E.A. Walsh, S.J., at the dedication of the E.A. Walsh Memorial Building, the new location for the School of Foreign Service, October, 1958. The Very Rev. Edward B. Bunn, S.J., president, Georgetown University, is looking on.

10. William Gaston of North Carolina

William Gaston of New Bern, North Carolina, was the first student who came to register at the Georgetown Academy on the hilltop, when it opened its doors to the public in 1791. His life story offers a noble example of an upright lawyer, conscientious judge, wise legislator, eloquent statesman, devoted patriot, faithful supporter of his original Alma Mater, and, above all, a sincere Catholic. In addition to carrying out his professional and legislative duties, he founded the first Catholic colony in a county in the western part of North Carolina, which was subsequently named for him. He was an eminently domestic man, who, after 1819, when widowed for the third time, devoted much of his leisure to the religious and moral training of his five children.

Throughout the years, Georgetown and its students have honored this outstanding man with a number of tributes: In his address at the 1888 Commencement, the Reverend James A. Doonan, S.J., president of the College, proposed that the name of this outstanding student be included in the designation of Georgetown's *aula maxima* in the Healy Building, to be known as "Gaston Memorial Hall." Also in his memory, one of the panels adorning the wall behind the stage bears Gaston's name under the sign of the scales of Justitia. In addition, preceding the commencement exercises in June 1894, "amidst a flourish of trumpets, Cardinal Gibbons unveiled the bust of Georgetown's proto-alumnus," which had been donated by his family. Although already used for festive occasions for a number of years, the official inauguration of "Gaston Memorial Hall" took place on November 4, 1901, and was celebrated with a concert given by the U.S. Marine Band. Furthermore, one of the junior debating clubs, founded in 1911, honored his memory by assuming his name.

Gaston Memorial Hall has welcomed many distinguished guests: Several Presidents of the United States have participated in commencement exercises; Eugenio Cardinal Pacelli, later to become Pius XII, visited here in 1936 to receive an honorary degree; and such speakers as Chancellor Adenauer, King Hussein of Jordan, Walter Reuther, and Nicky Giovanni graced its stage. It was there that the "Gaston Lectures," discussions of various subjects by distinguished speakers, were held. In the early 1930s, Father Walsh presented his lecture series there until their increasing popularity required relocation in 1937 to the more spacious Memorial Continental Hall in the DAR Building.

As we are celebrating this year and well into 1939, the Sesquicentennial of the Constitution of the United States, Georgetown University is commemorating a similar anniversary. These events come at a time when more than ever before the broad principles of government and the specific guarantees of fundamental human liberty are being flouted in many corners of the earth and are not immune from serious challenge even in the land of their origin. During the one hundred fifty years of their national existence under that organic law, the United States has achieved an enviable position among the nations of the earth; our country still ranks among the most stable, prosperous and powerful, in spite of the shocks to our national economy experienced during the last decade. Similiar—nay, lesser reverses—in other lands have had fatal consequences in the form of sanguinary revolutions, social chaos, national bankruptcy, dictatorships and the disappearance of many precious liberties, both civil and religious. The comparative immunity from fundamental upheaval which we have enjoyed in an age of universal disaster is not an accident. Neither is it a lucky chance due to some oversight of destiny or caprice of nature. Heavy though our material losses have been since 1929, appalling though the suffering may still be, and urgent though the problems are that face our democracy, the fabric of our national life is still sound and the traditional pattern of our political structure still stands unimpaired. That blessing is directly traceable to definite causes.

Speech delivered at the University of North Carolina, Chapel Hill, on November 28, 1938.

The American democracy rests upon a bedrock of stubborn vitality that is not satisfactorily or completely explained by referring to our geographic isolation from Europe, our tremendous natural resources, actual or potential wealth, inventive genius, resiliency of character or powers of quick recuperation after physical shock. Physical capacity to do a given task is not always guarantee for eventual performance. The enlightened mind and the obstinate will to victory are indispensable ingredients of success. Both mind and will are formed during the youthful days of men and of nations; the impress they then receive creates habits, and habits determine both character and conduct.

The character of the American political system was moulded by men who walked in greatness and faced destiny unafraid. Washington, Hancock, Jefferson, Hamilton, Madison, John Marshall, Benjamin Franklin, John Jay, James Wilson, the Lees of Virginia, the Carrolls of Maryland and the Adamses of Massachusetts. What a goodly fellowship of princely men with empires in their brains, wisdom on their lips and courage in their hands! They stood toe to toe with the most powerful military power of the day and flung their claims for liberty into the very teeth of a monarchical age. Rightly and justly could Lord Chatham say of them on the floor of the British Parliament: "...the men gathered in the Continental Congress at Philadelphia are the equal of any similar assembly in history."

Into such an atmosphere of high resolve and dynamic conflict William Gaston was born, on September 19, 1778, at New Bern in this State of North Carolina. The first air he breathed was instinct with embattled freedom and the first things he ever saw must have left their seal forever on his soul. As a child of three still clasped in his mother's arms, he witnesses the murder of his father by a band of Tories who had preceded the British regulars in the attack on New Bern. When the town had to be abandoned, Dr. Alexander Gaston, one of the most determined advocates of resistance to the British Crown and Parliament, was attempting to transport his family to a safer place, to his plantation on

Bryce's Creek, some eight miles distant. He had secured a boat of some sort and was standing upright in it, when the Tories who hated his uncompromising patriotism succeeded in preventing the embarkation of the entire family. The musket that deprived William Gaston of his patriot father was levelled directly over the shoulder of his distracted mother, as she knelt and implored compassion for her infant children and mercy for her husband.

Young Gaston's subsequent unswerving faith in democracy and his allegiance to the soil of North Carolina were thus baptized, as it were, in the blood of a father fallen in the cause of American independence. He never forgot that tragedy on the banks of the river Trent and often recalled its significance in the years of his maturity....

If his contribution to the upbuilding of the American democracy were analyzed, I think it would be found to spring from an amalgam of two cognate elements: a passionate but rational love of the United States and a deep, philosophical faith in the religion he professed. The blood of a Huguenot father of the Presbyterian faith and the piety of a Catholic mother blended to produce a son whose name in your State is high in honor and secure in time. If the son was a great man it was, by his own confession, because the mother was a great woman. Mrs. E.F. Ellett, in that graceful work *The Women of the American Revolution*, ranks her among the heroines of that generation and describes her as a saint whose "...footsteps seemed to touch the earth only to mark the track that leads to heaven."

I do not propose to burden you tonight with a detailed biographical sketch of William Gaston because the chronology of his life is not so important as the manner of his living it and the use he made of his 66 years among you. Suffice it to recall that he was the first student to enroll in Georgetown College, after its foundation in 1789, and that his memory is perpetuated in the classic auditorium which bears his name, as well as by a bust in marble and by an oil-painting in the hall of the debating society, "The Philodemic." I deem it a privilege, consequently, to return on this occasion to the soil of North Carolina and pay tribute to the memory of one of our most distinguished sons and to our proto-alumnus.

Our activities preserve the records of his academic success in the form of several remarkable commendations from the faculty. Thus, the President, Reverend Robert Plunkett, wrote to Gaston's mother in 1792: "Your son is the best scholar and most exemplary youth we have in Georgetown...."

As the classics—and the humanities in general—have ever held an honored place in the Georgetown curriculum, Gaston early acquired that literary form and wealth of historic and poetic allusion that characterized his style in later years, when he crossed swords with giants like Clay and Calhoun, both of whom had reason to remember his ready speech, his clarity of vision and his power in debate. Admitted to the bar at 20 years of age, he was elected in 1800, one year after he became of full age, a member of the Senate of North Carolina. Later on, he became speaker of the House of Commons, thus serving in both branches of your State Legislature where he wrote and guided to enactment some of the most important statutes in the history of this Commonwealth. His law regulating the descent of inheritances he regarded as one of the proudest achievements in his life.

Elected to the U.S. Congress from the New Bern district in 1813 and re-elected in 1815, he straightaway took rank with the best minds in the national legislature. It was a critical period in the life of the young Republic, then at war with Great Britain for the second time. The pro-French policy of Jefferson, the proposal of a war on Canada, and the Loan Bill of 1815, all found him prepared to speak his mind with fearlessness and brilliant argument.... And although Calhoun was a dominating figure, the prestige of his venerable service and his mastery in debate did not prevent Gaston from differing from him whenever conscience so dictated. The Loan Bill of 1815 was an administration measure, a "must" legislation, and Calhoun showed considerable annoyance at young Gaston's refusal to accept it as mandatory....Gaston's reply was an eloquent defense of a minority's right in Congress to oppose with reason and sincerity any adminstration on a question affecting the public welfare without incurring the stigma of being obstructionist or reactionary. Recalling historic events in France, he pointed out that if more opposition had been manifested against entrenched government there, less blood would have flowed when freedom was lost under the dictatorship of Napoleon and the succeeding Empire. "Faction is a demon" he said, "faction out of power is a demon unchained, faction vested with attributes of rule is a Moloch of destruction." His peroration on that occasion manifested an independence of mind and an integrity of allegiance to essential democracy that might still be spoken in 1939....

Once again, on the floor of the U.S. Congress, with the redoubtable Henry Clay as antagonist, Gaston developed the same important thesis in his celebrated attack on the tyranny of the "previous question." This parliamentary device which permitted a majority to limit debate and prevent amendments to measures advocated by the controlling party, had been very successfully used to carry out the policy of the adminstration. It was a form of cloture available to any individual member, and assured the majority of an affirmative vote whenever they decided to end a disagreeable or awkward situation. The Speaker of the House was Henry Clay, and under his driving personality much use had been made of it to stifle opposition and sterilize contrary opinion.

Mr. Stanford of North Carolina, moved that the offensive practice of the "previous question" be expunged, and was seconded by Mr. Randolph of Virginia. Gaston's memorable defense of free speech and minority rights was pronounced in Congress on Friday, January 19, 1816. I shall give you the essence of Gaston's argument as it constitutes one of the most masterful orations ever pronounced from the floor of Congress. Gaston pointed out that the method regarding the "previous question" as practiced in North Carolina was totally different from procedures identified by the same name elsewhere. He said that neither the British Parliament nor the early American Congress deprived a member of the right to amend the main question, until the "memorable night of the 27th of February, 1811." He then detailed the change that occurred in connection with a supplemental bill prohibiting commercial relations with Great Britain, which established the precedent for the subsequent use of the "previous question." He refuted the argument that "necessity" justified the innovation.... This was Gaston's finest and most enduring contribution to free government....

Henry Clay defended the practice but was answered by Gaston in a spirited defense of freedom of debate. There is nothing superior to it in that golden age of the British orators made immortal by Fox, the Elder Pitt, Burke, Canning and Walpole. Nor is there sounder law, more impeccable logic or precedent anywhere in Coke or Blackstone. It is the Magna Carta of free speech in America and deserves to be reprinted at this time; it is concrete vindication of the motto inscribed on the wall of the Philodemic Society at Georgetown: *Colit Societas Philodemica Eloquentiam Libertati Devinctam* (The Philodemic Society cultivates eloquence in the service of Liberty). [James] Kent, in his *Commentaries on American Law*, 4th edition, referred to it, on page 238, and, in a more informal communication, he spoke of it as follows: "I have read it again this morning and, permit me to say, it is a masterly and scientific legal and constitutional argument with the most diligent examination and keen, critical analysis of the documentary Authorities. It is an admirable Production."

Important speeches such as this—and they abound in the annals of the 13th and 14th Congresses—caused Daniel Webster to reply to an enquiry from a member of Congress from Ohio with respect to the greatest man during the War Congress of 1812-1815: "The greatest man was William Gaston," but he added, "I myself came in along after him."

Also during his service in the U.S. Congress, Gaston performed his great filial service to the Georgetown College which he had entered as a boy of thirteen. He introduced and piloted through the assigned committees a Bill conferring authority on the College to award such academic degrees, honors and titles as were customarily granted by universities and other learned institutions. Passed by both House and Senate, the charter was signed by President Madison on March 1, 1815, the very day on which the President signed the Treaty of Peace negotiated between England and the United States at Ghent. Thus, it was largely due to the loyal affection of this first student, from North Carolina, that the College, founded on the banks of the Potomac by Carroll of Maryland, kinsman of the Catholic signer of the Declaration of Independence, became a University, destined in the succeeding centuries to grow in size and in public service to the constitutional democracy that had been born in the same year as Georgetown, 1789. Hence we both are celebrating our sesquicentennial this year.

If Gaston's services to the growing Republic were notable on the national stage, his subsequent contributions to the building up of his native state were equally distinguished and far reaching. After serving in the U.S. Congress, he returned to private practice in his home state, but his brilliant mind and superior character could not long escape being drafted for the public good. Within a year we see him a member of the State Senate and Chairman of the Judiciary Committee. It was in this capacity that he prepared the bill organizing and creating the Supreme Court of his state. As member of the legislature of North Carolina he made his historic defense of the banks of North Carolina in the crisis of 1828. Day by day he resisted the growing panic and succeeded in saving the banks from destruction and the State from disgrace. His defense of the old Constitution of North Carolina, in 1831, is especially recalled by the biographer of Gaston in *The National Portrait Gallery of Distinguished Americans*: "The constitution of the state is a venerable instrument. It came down to the present generation, from the sages of the revolution, and is loved and venerated in North Carolina for its very antiquity. It was a fit subject for the exhibition of his learning, eloquence, and patriotism, and those resources of his mind he poured forth with the most brilliant profusion."

It was this period of intense legal activity that made Gaston *facile princeps* in the legal profession of his State and, possibly, in the whole land, and caused the University of Pennsylvania, Columbia College, Harvard, and Princeton to honor him as a Doctor of Laws....

It was reported at the time that the Chief Justice of the United States, the great John Marshall, had said he would willingly resign if he could be sure that William Gaston of North Carolina would be appointed to succeed him.

I have rarely found an instance in our early history of a man so universally respected and loved, a circumstance that is doubly significant by reason of the fact that Gaston, a fervent and uncompromising Catholic, merited this high tribute in a community and in an age that was predominantly Protestant. John Marshall, obliged as were all the justices of the Supreme Court, to ride circuit and hear cases far from Washington, relied heavily on Gaston's judgment in his district. Many of Marshall's decisions were prepared by Gaston but delivered by the Chief Justice himself.

Profound jurist that he was, Gaston retained the broad humanity that distinguishes culture and wisdom from mere factual knowledge. As judge of the North Carolina Supreme Court, he spent may hours driving hither and yon throughout the state. Horse and buggy afforded him much time for contemplation and wide readings. It was his custom to carry the latest publications with him, so that, in the words of one writer: "...he was not unfrequently aroused from the enchantment of Scott or Irving by the upsetting of his sulky."

For 42 years he was a trustee of the University of North Carolina and took a very practical interest in education, even to the extent of visiting the classes one morning as early as 6 o'clock! Obviously, that was before the era of night permissions and fraternity life on the campus. His address to the graduates of the University of North Carolina's Commencement of 1832 is a profound exposition of the value and method of a liberal education as opposed to premature specialization before the mind has been disciplined by history, mathematics, the natural sciences, literature, the fine arts, logic and philosophy. It was a plea by a seasoned and balanced man of the world for the education of the whole man, not of departmentalized specialists eminent in one branch of knowledge, but crippled in their myopic inability to see life steadily and see it whole. With almost prophetic vision Gaston warned his day and generation against those very evils which education today deplores, but for which education is to blame, for its irrational worship of that mechanical monstrosity called the credit system under which the intangible and elusive qualities of a gentleman and a scholar are weighted and evaluated in terms of standardized mysteries called semester hours. I venture to assert that Gaston—nay, even Plato and Aristotle—would be routed out of any modern dean's office because of failure to produce a transcript proving their ability to sit through 120 semester hours. It was in this same address that Judge Gaston manifested his deep political wisdom and his fears for the future of the Southern States. He warned his listeners of the evils of slavery with a courage that is positive only when one loves passionately. "It is remarkable" writes Dr. Battle, "that when the public mind was inflamed peculiarly on account of the bloody insurrection of Nat Turner in the preceding year, the orator should have frankly avowed himself an advocate of the ultimate abolition of slavery and the audience cheered the utterance. This bold language did not weaken his influence."...

That commencement address of 1832 would merit a detailed analysis which time prevents at this hour. I can only commend it to your attention and refer you to the high opinion expressed on it both by Chief Justice John Marshall and Dr. [Kemp P.] Battle in the *History of the University of North Carolina*, Vol. I, p. 344. The address ran through 5 editions and was reprinted as late as 1858 by the two literary bodies of this University, the Philanthropic and Dialectic Societies.

But Gaston was not only a theorist with no practice. We cherish in our archives at Georgetown the following communication in regard to a negro slave, addressed to the Jesuits at St. Inigoes, Maryland:

> "I place my boy Augustus under the charge of the Rev. Joseph Carbury to receive moral and religious instruction, to be taught a useful trade, and, when qualified to make a fit use of his freedom, to be emancipated. September 1, 1824, William Gaston."

It was in 1833 that Gaston's crowning service was rendered to the State of North Carolina and to the cause of religious freedom in the whole country. The Supreme Court of the State had been under fire by politicians anxious to minimize its influence and nullify the checks it interposed against unsound legislation. On the death of Chief Justice Henderson, Gaston was importuned by thoughtful leaders of all beliefs to accept the office of Justice, for he alone, they all agreed, could save the Supreme Court by the universal respect he enjoyed in all quarters. After conquering his private financial objections, Gaston still found himself confronted by a serious problem—article 32 of the then prevailing Constitution of 1776, which read: "That no person who shall deny the being of God, or the truth of the Protestant Religion...shall be capable of holding any office or place of trust or profit in the civil department within this state." Devout and practising Catholic that he was, Gaston was finally persuaded that this prohibition so contradicted other controlling guarantees in the same North Carolina Constitution that no legal impediment remained to his acceptance. This was the opinion of such learned jurists as Chief Justice Ruffin of North Carolina, Chief Justice John Marshall of the Supreme Court of the United States, and Governor Swain, the then Chief Executive of the State.

The legal opinions were based on the Bill of Rights of the North Carolina Constitution of 1776, Section 19, which declared "...that all men have a natural and unalienable right to worship Almighty God according to the dictates of their own conscience." And the 34th section of the Constitution provided "...that there shall be no establishment of any religious church or denomination in this State, in preference to any other." Since these contradictory declarations emanated from the same source and since two were categoric and only one seemingly discriminatory, the more literal construction prevailed. Gaston finally accepted and became a powerful judge whose opinions have passed into history and were frequently cited in legal controversies elsewhere.

A convention to amend and modernize the old Constitution was called in 1835, and convened in June at Raleigh. It was then that Judge Gaston, sitting for New Bern, rose on the question of amending or striking out the odious discrimination against Catholics contained in the 32nd clause, and in dramatic tension pronounced an oration that remained to this day the classic defense in American history of religious liberty and freedom of conscience. For two days he riveted the attention of the convention on his carefully prepared statement of the ghastly consequences of religious intolerance and bigotry in public life.

In the full zenith of his splendid intellect he marshalled page after page of history, dogma and doctrine before his respectful and attentive colleagues. The text might be simply redated as of today and dispatched to Soviet Russia and Nazi Germany in defense of Catholics, Protestants and Jews, oppressed by the new paganism of modern times. It ranks with the best in Newman's defense of Catholic loyalty and in Daniel O'Connell's Emancipation oratory. Drawing copiously on American history, he cited the three pioneers in the field of religious freedom: Lord Baltimore, the Catholic in the foundation of the Maryland colony; Roger Williams, the Baptist founder of the free community of Rhode Island, and William Penn, the Quaker founder of Pennsylvania. Then he recalled the liberal attitude of Washington in his reply to the Catholics of the United States on the occasion of their letter of felicitations to the first President.

Gaston's closing sentences made a deep impression on the Convention!

"The proscriptive denunciation contained in this Article, whether it could or could not be enforced, never has been enforced. The question before us is one, not of practical convenience, but of fundamental principles. He who would sacrifice such principles to the passion or caprice or excitement of the moment, may be called a politician, but he is no Statesman. We are now examining into the soundness of the foundation of our institutions. If we rest the fabric of the Constitution upon prejudices, unreasoning and mutable prejudices, we build upon sand; but let us lay it on the broad and firm basis of natural right, equal justice and universal freedom—freedom of opinion—freedom, civil and religious—freedom as approved by the wise, and sanctioned by the good—and then may we hope that it shall stand against the storms of faction, violence and injustice, then we shall have founded it upon a ROCK."

His citation of the work of Bancroft brought a letter of thanks from the historian in which he expressed gratitude for such honorable mention and pride for having been summoned as witness in such a cause, and "Still more, what I value more highly than praise from a man whose name I have never mentioned but with praise, is that what I had written furnished an argument favorable to intellectual liberty. It is the highest reward to which I could have aspired."

To the eternal credit of the people of North Carolina the offensive discrimination was removed by a majority vote and Gaston returned to his bench to continue for nearly ten years his distinguished service to justice and to the interpretation, application and defense of the American democracy. His chief life work was done and nobly done. On his death in January 1844, he left a memory to be cherished with reverence by his country, his State and his church.

Chronology of Father Walsh's Life

1885   Born October 10 in South Boston, youngest of six children of Irish immigrants.

1902   Entered the Society of Jesus in Frederick, Maryland.

1909   After studies at Woodstock College, Maryland, awarded B.A. degree by Georgetown University.

Appointed instructor at Georgetown University.

1912-1914   Continued studies at National University, Dublin, London University, and University of Innsbruck, Austria.

1916   Ordained to the priesthood at Woodstock College, Maryland, by James Cardinal Gibbons.

1917   Awarded M.A. degree at Woodstock College, Maryland.

1918   Appointed Dean of the College of Arts and Sciences, Georgetown University.

Selected as member of Special Commission of the War Department to administer the Student Army Training Corps (SATC). Served as Assistant Educational Director of the SATC in Corps Area I, the New England States.

1919   Founded the School of Foreign Service as a department of Georgetown University and became its first Regent.

1922-1923   By appointment of Pope Pius XI, served as Director-General of the Papal Relief Mission to Soviet Russia and Vatican Representative concerning church interests in the Soviet Union.

1924 Started his public lecture series at the Smithsonian Institution.

1927 Appointed President of the Catholic Near East Welfare Association by Pope Pius XI for five years.

1929 Selected by Pope Pius XI to a three-man special committee, Father Walsh successfully negotiated settlement of the conflict between the Mexican Government and the Roman Catholic Church.

1931 Delegated by the Vatican, Father Walsh examined the possibility of setting up a Catholic school in Baghdad, Iraq, and succeeded in obtaining agreement from the government of Iraq for the establishment of an American College in Baghdad.

1935 and 1939 Presented a series of lectures, in French, at the Académie de Droit International de la Haye, The Hague.

1939-1940 Organized and administered the Finnish Relief Fund in Washington, D.C.

1945-1946 Served as consultant to the U.S. Chief of Counsel, Supreme Court Justice Robert H. Jackson, at the International Military Tribunal in Nuremberg.

1946 Appointed member of the U.S. President's Advisory Commission on Universal Military Training.

1947-1948 Appointed by Father General as Official Visitor to the Japanese Mission of the Society of Jesus to study educational and religious issues.

1949 In cooperation with Professor Léon Dostert, organized the Institute of Languages and Linguistics at Georgetown University.

1952 Celebrated his Golden Jubilee in the Society of Jesus.

1956 Died October 31.

Father Walsh received honorary degrees of Doctor of Laws from the University of Delaware (1934), the University of Detroit (1938), St. Joseph's College, Philadelphia (1943), and of Doctor of Literature from Georgetown University (1936).

Decorations received from foreign governments include the Medal of Public Instruction (Venezuela 1921), the Cross of Merit (Chile 1933), the

Cross of the White Rose (Finland 1941) and the Verdienstkreuz (Federal Republic of Germany, 1953).

Publications of E.A. Walsh, S.J.

1928   *The Fall of the Russian Empire* (Little, Brown, and Company).

1931   *The Last Stand* (Little, Brown, and Company).

1934   *Ships and National Safety* (Georgetown University School of Foreign Service).

1935   *The Woodcarver of Tyrol* (Harper and Brothers Publishers).

1948   *Total Power* (Doubleday & Company, Inc.).

1951   *Total Empire* (The Bruce Publishing Company).

* * *

1922   *The History and Nature of International Relations*, editor (The Macmillan Company).

1942   *The Political Economy of Total War*, co-author with W.S. Culbertson (The Macmillan Company).

1945   Article on "Geopolitics and International Morals" in *Compass of the World*, ed. Hans W. Wigert and V. Stefansson (The Macmillan Company).

"Les Principes Fondamentaux de la Vie Internationale" and "L'Evolution de la Diplomatie aux Etats Unis" (lectures given at the Académie de Droit International de la Haye in 1935 and 1939, respectively, published in *Receuil des Cours*, vols. 59 and 63).

Numerous magazine articles on Soviet Russia, geopolitics, and international relations.

In addition, Father Walsh delivered a number of radio addresses and sermons.